DIRECTIONS IN DEVELOPMENT

Unions and Collective Bargaining

Economic Effects in a Global Environment

Toke Aidt
Zafiris Tzannatos

THE WORLD BANK
Washington, D.C.

ISBN 0-8213-5080-3

Library of Congress Cataloging-in-Publication Data has been applied for.

Contents

Tables, Figures, and Boxes

Foreword

The form industrial relations take in different countries can be critical in balancing competitiveness with concern for fairer wages and better working conditions. Accepting that workers should have a fair share of the benefits associated with economic growth without being penalized for crises for which they are not responsible is not just another view of looking at globalization; it is the very essence of humanity. This is not a new idea it can be traced back to the Aristotelian notion that a good government is one whose policies and actions are determined by justice and common interest.

While history shows that there can be periods of balanced economic and social outcomes, a variety of short-run effects of unionism may exist simultaneously. Approaching these issues with rhetoric dichotomies (such as, "Are unions good or bad?") is not constructive. This book reviews the extensive literature on trade unions not just from the conventional quantitative lens of unionization rates (for example, how many workers are unionized) but from the broader perspective of how workers and employers interact in a dynamic economy, and what role the government has in such a setting. Broadening the analysis in this way shows that the relationship between economic performance and different economic settings, industrial relations, and governmental policies is often blurred and certainly nonlinear. While full employment, wage adequacy, and quality of work can certainly coexist (as in the case of many OECD economies), history also suggests that these three desirable aspects sometimes emerge at the expense of others. For example, fast employment generation is often associated with wage levels and employment conditions that give rise to social concerns. At the same time, fast internationalization of production can imply declining power of governments to pursue autonomous national policies. Does the answer to these problems rest with the type and extent of coordination among the social partners? If so, to what extent can coordination be confined within national boundaries and statutes, and what is the role of transnational organizations and international agreements?

There are no simple answers to these questions. And the current study does not attempt to provide unambiguous conclusions where they do not exist. However, it provides the much needed basis for understanding economic performance not just in the presence of trade unions but in the broader context of industrial relations. My own conclusion from the study is that coordination among social partners can promote better investment climates while also fostering a fairer distribution of output.

Mamphela Ramphele
Managing Director for
    Human Development
World Bank

Foreword

Providing equitable and inclusive labor markets is one of the most important components of social protection. This is one of the central conclusions of the World Bank's recent (2001) *Social Protection Sector Strategy: From Safety Net to Springboard*. Since labor is often a poor person's main or only asset, equitable access to safe and well-paid employment is a key method of reducing the risk of unemployment and poverty for individuals. Formalization of the labor relationship is reflected in labor standards, including the freedom of association and the right to collective bargaining. Sound industrial relations between employers and employees can lead to a stable economy and prevent settlements that are detrimental to the functioning of the economy. To achieve this potential win-win outcome, developing labor standards needs to go hand in hand with building institutional capacity and trust between workers, employers, and the government. The need for workers, employers, and governments to find solutions that reduce poverty through both growth and distributional efficiency is becoming increasingly important in an era of rapid globalization.

The World Bank is committed to approaching issues surrounding labor market standards on a pragmatic, country-by-country basis. The Bank supports the promotion of all core labor standards in many ways. It offers training to its staff on these issues, engages in regular dialogue with trade unions, fosters partnerships with other international organizations working on these issues, and conducts research. The Bank is working to build up its knowledge base in this area and learn from the experience of partner institutions and the international community.

This book is part of this broader effort. It examines the economic effects of trade unions and collective bargaining by looking at the international evidence on the micro- and macroeconomic impacts of unions and different bargaining institutions in a comparative cross-country context. The study is based on a large and detailed literature survey covering more than 1,000 primary and secondary studies. It is aimed at taking stock of existing knowledge on these issues in order to pave the way for a better understanding of this subject in the future. We hope that the information presented here stimulates research and dialogue in this very important area.

Robert Holzmann
Director, Social Protection
World Bank

Preface and Acknowledgments

Although the massive literature on the effects of unionism ought to identify some central tendency, the results of this research are often quoted selectively. This book therefore aims to provide a systematic and synthetic review of the global research on the economic effects of unions and collective bargaining at the micro- and macroeconomic levels. Earlier drafts of the manuscript were shared extensively among peers and at meetings, including a major international conference in Geneva in November 2000. This book incorporates recent developments in the literature, as well as feedback and valuable additions from many international organizations and workers'/employers' representatives as well as World Bank staff. Nevertheless, the literature on labor standards, collective bargaining, and trade unions is developing rapidly in many directions and we apologize for any omissions. We would like to thank, without implicating for any errors, Gordon Betcherman, Amit Dar, Peter Fallon, Morley Gunderson, Robert Holzmann, Steen Jorgensen, William Martin, Martin Rama, Sabine Schlemmer-Schulte, and Vania Sena for comments on early versions of the manuscript. We would also like to thank the World Bank's Office of the Publisher for its advice on improving this publication. The study was supported by the Social Protection Department of the World Bank's Human Development Network and by Danish Trust Funds.

Zafiris Tzannatos
Washington, D.C.

Toke Aidt
Cambridge, U.K.

December, 2001

About the Authors

Toke Aidt is a member of the Faculty of Economics and Politics, University of Cambridge, U.K. His research interests include labor market institutions and political economics, and previous publications include articles in *Journal of Public Economics*, *Public Choice*, and *Economics and Politics*, among others.

Zafiris Tzannatos is currently adviser to the World Bank's managing director for human development. He has worked widely on social protection issues in the Middle East and North Africa and led the Bank's Global Child Labor Program. Prior to joining the World Bank, he held a series of senior academic posts in Europe and served as an advisor to governments and international organizations. He has published widely in the areas of applied economics, gender, education, and children.

Acronyms

CGE	computable general equilibrium
EPZ	export processing zone
GDP	gross domestic product
GLS	generalized least squares
GNP	gross national product
ILO	International Labour Organization
NMR	negative monotonic relationship
NR	no relationship
OECD	Organisation for Economic Co-operation and Development
OLS	ordinary least squares
R&D	research and development
PMR	positive monotonic relationship
WLS	weighted least squares

1

Introduction and Summary

This book examines the economic effects of unions and collective bargaining. Although the study is based on a large and detailed literature survey (covering more than 1,000 primary and secondary studies), it cannot claim to be conclusive. The main contribution is to take stock of existing knowledge, thereby paving the way for more innovative future research on the link between labor standards, collective bargaining, and economic performance. The specific findings of our study are summarized in this chapter, which also offers some additional remarks on what can be learned from our reading of the literature.

Governments around the world and international organizations such as the Organisation for Economic Co-operation and Development (OECD) and the World Bank (World Bank, 1995) have in recent years become aware that labor standards are a potentially important determinant of economic performance. By labor standards we mean the rules that govern working conditions and industrial relations. The precise link between labor standards and economic performance is as yet not clear and many controversies remain, but the fact is that labor standards now appear on the international agenda and are likely to stay there for a foreseeable future.

One of the driving forces behind the current interest in labor standards around the world is the expansion of international trade and the liberalization of financial markets—sometimes known as globalization—that has occurred during the past decades. As globalization proceeds, differences in labor standards between countries and regions arguably become more important than they used to be. This is not only because such differences might give a cost advantage in internationally traded goods to countries with low standards, but also because new technology enables labor services to be directly subcontracted to workers in low-standard countries. For example, a number of data entry procedures are performed in the Caribbean for U.S.–based companies and are transmitted to them electronically. Another example is the work carried out by skilled Indian engineers who receive initial drawings from American companies by satellite and send the final products back to the United States in the same way. Thus, labor standards can no longer be the concern only of individual governments but must also become a concern of the international community. The need for international engagement is also highlighted by the fact that individual countries often have very different views on what constitute proper labor standards and what the consequences of adopting them might be. One view holds that labor regulation reduces economic efficiency and growth, and as this is more important for countries with a high incidence of poverty, this view is often held by developing countries (Herzenberg 1990). Another view often found among industrial countries is that differences in labor regulation tend to discriminate against those countries that have higher standards and greater respect for workers' rights. The United States, for example, regards violations of basic workers' rights and minimum labor standards as unfair trade practices. It has adopted legislation to this effect (such as the Omnibus Trade and Competitiveness Act of 1988) that restricts trade and investment guarantees in countries that either do not enforce or violate labor rights and standards (Perez-Lopez 1988, 1990).

The International Labour Organisation (ILO) defines five *core* labor standards: (a) the prohibition of slavery and compulsory labor, (b) the elimination of discrimination, (c) the prohibition of exploitative child labor, (d) freedom of association (the right of workers to form unions of their own choice and of employers to form employers' organizations), and (e) the right to collective bargaining (the right of unions and employers' organizations to negotiate work conditions on behalf of workers and employers, respectively).

Among these standards, the right to collective bargaining and the right to freedom of association probably give rise to the most controversy, and they are the focus of this book. A recent OECD study (OECD 1996) has revealed significant differences in the extent to which these two standards are "guaranteed by law and practice" across a large sample of developing and industrial countries. The study divides countries into four groups as shown in table 1-1. The countries in group 1 are those that permit freedom of association and collective bargaining, and include almost all the OECD countries. The countries in groups 2 and 3 place some restrictions on workers' rights, while the countries in group 4 seriously suppress these rights.

The classification in table 1-1 points to enormous differences around the world, not only in workers' rights but also in the organization and

Table 1-1.   Labor Standards in Selected Countries, 1970–94

Group number	Definition	Countries
Group 1	Freedom of association, on the whole, is guaranteed by law and practice.	All OECD countries, except the Republic of Korea, Mexico, and Turkey. In addition, Bahamas, Barbados, Israel, Malta, and Suriname.
Group 2	Some restrictions exist, but it is possible to establish independent workers' organizations and union confederations.	Argentina, Brazil, Chile, Ecuador, Ethiopia, Fiji, Hong Kong, India, Jamaica, Mexico, Niger, Papua New Guinea, Peru, South Africa, República Bolivariana de Venezuela, and Zambia.
Group 3	Restrictions on freedom of association are significant, that is, stringent registration requirements exist, and political interference or acts of antiunion discrimination make it very difficult to form independent workers' organizations or union confederations.	Algeria, Bangladesh, Bolivia, Taiwan (China), Colombia, Ghana, Guatemala, Honduras, Kenya, Mali, Malaysia, Morocco, Nigeria, Pakistan, Philippines, Sri Lanka, Thailand, Tunisia, Turkey, and Zimbabwe.
Group 4	Freedom of association is practically nonexistent.	Cameroon, China, Egypt, Indonesia, Iran, Kuwait, Syria, and Tanzania.

Source: OECD (1996).

conduct of industrial relations more generally. A casual look at the table moreover suggests huge differences in the standard of living particularly between the countries in group 1 and 4, and not surprisingly OECD (1996) does find a positive correlation between GDP per capita and compliance with the two labor standards. Although it is clear that this cannot be ascribed to differences in workers' rights alone, it does raise an interesting and very important question: what is the link between labor standards and economic performance?

The purpose of this book is to investigate this question. To this end, we ask what can be learned from existing economic literature about the economic consequences of adopting or enforcing the two labor standards. It turns out that very little systematic evidence exists on this question.

This is partly due to the fact that it is very hard to isolate the contribution of these labor standards from other determinants of economic performance in cross-country studies and partly due the fact that it is hard to measure differences in labor standards across time and space. Some progress has, however, been made, and we examine the evidence in chapter 2. The remainder of the book focuses on two more specific questions: what is the impact on the economic well-being of individual workers and the performance of firms of basing industrial relations on collective bargaining between unions and employers rather than relying on individual contracting (question A) and what is the impact on the macroeconomy of adopting different institutional approaches to collective bargaining (question B). It is our hope that answering questions A and B will improve our understanding of the merits of the two underlying labor standards, and provide a starting point for future research aimed directly at clarifying the link between labor standards and economic performance.

Questions A and B have been thoroughly researched by economists, industrial relations scholars, and political scientists, and there exists a vast literature on the subject. In chapter 3, we briefly discuss the relevant theoretical literature related to unions, employers' organizations, and collective bargaining. This provides the theoretical background for what follows in chapters 4 and 5. In chapter 4, we examine what microeconometric studies of union behavior and collective bargaining at the firm and industry level can tell us about question A. In chapter 5, we change the focus and examine how different systems of collective bargaining affect macroeconomic performance (question B).

The Findings of the Book

The rest of this chapter is devoted to a summary of our findings. We begin with three general observations:

1. Comparative studies reveal little systematic difference in economic performance between countries that enforce the two relevant labor standards and countries that do not. This is partly a reflection of the difficulties of isolating the effects of labor standards from other determinants of economic performance, and suggests that the impact of labor standards perhaps best can be analyzed on a case-by-case basis.
2. The microeconomic consequences of collective bargaining are context–specific, and although unions in both industrial and developing countries are successful in securing a wage markup for their members and other workers covered by collective agreements, no general conclusions about the *net* costs (or benefits) of

unions can be reached. Depending on the economic, institutional, and political environment in which unions and employers interact, collective bargaining as opposed to individual contracting can contribute negatively or positively to the economic performance of firms and to the well-being of workers.

3. The macroeconomic impact of collective bargaining is hard to disentangle from other determinants of economic performance. While the available evidence from comparative studies of the OECD countries is fragile, two general features should be emphasized. First, the impact of collective bargaining on various aspects of macroeconomic performance depends on the economic, legal, and political environment in which collective bargaining takes place and can vary over time. Second, important complementarities exist between key aspects of the bargaining system. Therefore, the impact of individual aspects such as union density or centralization of bargaining cannot be assessed in isolation. It is the package of institutions that matters.

We elaborate on these themes in the following two sections where we attempt to summarize in more detail the specific findings related to questions A and B.

Findings Regarding Question A (Microeconomic Effects)

The human rights argument in support of workers' rights is compelling. But from an economic point of view the key questions are: What are the costs and benefits of unions? Is collective bargaining a useful institution that contributes to the achievement of desirable economic outcomes at the firm and/or sector level, or is it another labor market distortion that prevents the market from doing its job?

The existence of unions arises from the asymmetry in contracting between individual workers and employers, the concern for basic workers' rights, and the different perceptions about the merits of employment relations governed by individual contracts or collective agreements. Textbook reasoning suggests that the alternative to a unionized labor market is one characterized by the atomistic, perfectly competitive structure that ensures that individual workers choose whether or not to work by comparing the given perfectly competitive wage with the marginal utility of nonmarket activity. However, the reality facing policymakers is far less clear-cut than this suggests. First, the "removal" of unions may not reveal an underlying perfectly competitive situation in the labor market; instead, it may expose market imperfections on the labor demand side in the form of monopsony, that is, a situation in which there is only one buyer of the relevant labor services. Alternatively, firms in some industries may voluntarily pay workers more than the going market rate to motivate existing workers or to attract new ones. Hence, policy decisions whose central objective is the "return" to a perfectly competitive labor market (with all its well-known potential benefits) can succeed only if they are accompanied by policies designed to free up the demand side of the market. Indeed, the presence of unions in such circumstances may offer a second-best alternative to free competition. In this case, the countervailing influence of unions may result in a set of outcomes closer to the competitive equilibrium than those that would result from competition on the supply side of the labor market and monopsony on the demand side. The removal of unions may also reveal imperfections on the supply side of the labor market unrelated to unionism. For example, workers with specific skills or those protected by high turnover costs can gain "insider power," which can be used to raise wages above the competitive level. Moreover, the potential benefits (referred to as participatory benefits) associated with the presence of unions in the form of "voice" (empowerment) as opposed to "exit" (separation) effects should be counted against the costs (in the form of welfare losses due to misallocation effects). We see that theoretical reasoning does not allow us to reach unambiguous conclusions about the net benefits (or cost) of unions. Whether collective bargaining contributes to the achievement of desirable economic outcomes or it prevents the market from doing its job is, at the end of the day, an empirical question.

To evaluate the costs and benefits of unions empirically, we need, in principle, to know how the labor market would work in their absence. The counterfactual is, of course, never observable in reality, nor can it, as argued above, be deduced from theory. Therefore, evaluations of the costs and benefits of unions must necessarily be based on a comparison of economic outcomes in those sectors of the economy that are unionized with those that are not, rather than comparing outcomes in currently unionized sectors with the likely outcomes if those sectors had not been unionized. In practice, this is done by estimating a union/nonunion differential or markup from individual worker or establishment data. The union/nonunion differential is the difference between the target variable (wages, employment growth, productivity, and so on) in an average unionized firm (for a unionized worker) and an average nonunionized firm (for a nonunionized worker). Much of the empirical evidence on union/nonunion markups comes from the United States and the United Kingdom, but studies from other industrial countries as well as from some developing countries do exist, and are included in our survey.

We summarize the findings in 23 separate points. To aid exposition, we have grouped the findings into several related subject areas, preceded by an explanatory statement and a judgment about the robustness of the particular findings. The first group of findings relates to the wage markup; these results are very robust.

1. Union members and other workers covered by collective agreements in industrial as well as in developing countries do, on average, get a wage markup over their nonunionized (or uncovered) counterparts.
2. The markup is somewhat larger in the United States (15 percent) than in most other industrial countries (5 to 10 percent). In developing and middle-income countries, the markup can be higher or lower. For example, it appears high in Ghana, Malaysia, Mexico, and South Africa but relatively low in the Republic of Korea (in 1988, before the expansion of unionism).
3. Unions compress the wage distribution. In particular, the wage differentials between skilled and unskilled workers and the private return to education are reduced when unions are present.
4. One, albeit incomplete, way to assess the adverse effects of unions is to evaluate the welfare loss that the wage markup creates through the misallocation of resources in the whole economy. In general, these effects have been found to be small and of comparable magnitude to the deadweight loss arising from monopolies in product markets—no more than 0.2 to 0.5 percent of gross domestic product (GDP). However, even these low estimates may overstate the allocative loss of unions because they do not take full account of the unions' potential effects on the productivity of their members (see points 21-23). On the other hand, they do not include all the potential costs of unions, such as the adverse impact that unions may have on firms' investment behavior, so the estimates may understate the allocative loss of unionism (see point 20).

The size of the wage markup depends on a variety of worker and workplace characteristics. These include the following:

5. There is no significant difference between the wage markup for female workers and that for male workers in the United States and Australia. In some other countries such as Germany, Japan, Mexico, South Africa, and, perhaps, the United Kingdom, however, unionized women workers have a greater pay advantage over their nonunionized counterparts than unionized men.
6. There is some evidence from Canada and Malaysia to suggest that unions contribute to a reduction in the overall gender pay gap. British studies on the subject are inconclusive.
7. In the United States and the United Kingdom, unionized nonwhite workers tend to get a higher wage markup than white

workers, although the U.S. evidence is mixed. In South Africa, "black" unions are associated with a smaller markup than "white" unions. In Mexico and Canada, unions have been found to reduce the discrimination against indigenous people.

8. The wage markup tends to be higher in the private sector than in the public sector in industrial countries.

 The markup also depends on the economic environment in which unions and firms operate.

9. The impact of competitive conditions at the product market on the wage markup is not clear-cut and depends on how the competitiveness of the product market is measured. When firm-specific indicators of the competitive environment are used, unions are more successful in establishing a high wage markup if the relevant firms operate under less competitive conditions in the product market. This is not the case if industry concentration ratios are used as an indicator of product market competition. Arguably firm-specific indicators of competition are preferable to industry-wide indicators and so, on balance, product market competition seems to prevent unions from establishing a high wage markup.

Finally, the size of the wage markup also depends on the specific aspects of how collective bargaining is organized, and from the evidence it is possible to identify particular aspects of industrial relations that add to the markup.

10. Industries with high overall union density tend to have a higher wage markup.

11. Although in some countries, such as Malaysia and the United States, industry-level collective bargaining is associated with a higher markup than firm-level bargaining, this is not so in other countries. For example, recent studies from the United Kingdom fail to find a difference.

12. Multiunionism at the firm level (when different unions compete to recruit or organize the same workers) does not lead to a higher markup per se. However, evidence from the United Kingdom shows that the markup is high in multiunion firms that negotiate separately with each union.

13. Pre-entry closed shops (union membership is a prerequisite to obtain employment) but not post-entry closed shops (union membership is required after hiring) are associated with an additional wage markup. Again, this evidence comes from the United Kingdom only.

The union impact on aspects of economic performance other than wages is less well understood. Although a number of conclusions can be drawn with some certainty, most should be treated as tentative. The most robust results relate to hours worked, job mobility, and profitability.

14. Voluntary job turnover is lower and job tenure longer in union-ized firms. The evidence on this finding from Australia, Japan, Malaysia, the United Kingdom, and the United States seems quite robust. On the other hand, layoffs, particularly temporary lay-offs, are more frequent in unionized firms than in nonunionized ones.

15. Net company profits (price-cost ratios, Tobin's q, subjective prof-itability assessments, and the like) tend to be lower in unionized firms than in similar nonunionized firms (in Japan, the United Kingdom, and the United States). There seems to be a relatively large negative impact on profitability in firms that have product market power.

16. Hours worked is lower among unionized than nonunionized workers. This is true for both total and normal hours. In addi-tion, unionized workers are more likely to get paid for the over-time work that they do.

The evidence concerning employment-related benefits, spending on research and development (R&D) and physical investment, and employ-ment growth is less robust, but the following could be noted.

17. Fringe benefits are more commonly found among unionized workers than among nonunionized ones (in Australia, Japan, Ma-laysia, the United Kingdom, and the United States). Benefits can include severance pay, paid holidays, paid sick leave, pension plans, and so on. At the same time, there is evidence that part of the wage markup is compensation for an inflexible and struc-tured work environment.

18. Employment growth can be slower in unionized than in nonunionized firms (as suggested by evidence from Canada, Ja-maica, Malaysia, the United Kingdom, and the United States), but the evidence is not particularly strong, and the observed dif-ferences most likely represent situations of disequilibrium.

19. Although spending on R&D tends to be lower in unionized than in nonunionized firms, unionized firms seem to adopt new tech-nology as fast as nonunionized ones (in Canada, Malaysia, the United Kingdom, and the United States).

20. The investment rate (physical capital) tends to be lower in union-ized than in nonunionized firms with otherwise similar

characteristics (in the United Kingdom and the United States). The adverse impact seems to be relatively larger when firms operate in competitive product markets, although only one study (from the United Kingdom) has addressed this issue directly.

The least robust results relate to productivity, training, and pay systems.

21. The impact of unions on productivity levels (in terms of both labor productivity and total factor productivity) is empirically indeterminate. Some studies suggest a positive impact, but others imply a negative impact or no impact at all. For example, unions appear to have a negative impact on productivity levels in the United Kingdom but a positive impact in Malaysia. In the United States, there is no discernible impact, on average, but there is considerable variation across industries. Industries operating in competitive product markets and firms with "high quality" industrial relations (as measured by grievances among workers, strikes, and the like) have, on average, high productivity.

22. The relationship between unions and productivity growth is not clear either. In the United States, the union/nonunion differential is found to be negative or insignificant. In the United Kingdom, some studies suggest that the weakening of British unions is one factor explaining the high productivity growth in the United Kingdom in the 1980s.

23. Unionized workers tend to receive more training than their nonunionized counterparts, especially company-related training.

Overall, these findings show that the extent to which particular costs prevail or particular benefits materialize depends on the economic environment in which unions and employers operate, as well as the way in which collective bargaining is organized. It is of primary interest to note that specific aspects of the economic and institutional environment, such as product market competition, absence of pre-entry closed shops and so on, can help to minimize the net costs or maximize the net benefits of unions. In devising union regulations, policymakers must recognize this fact and seek to remove the costs of unions while at the same time retaining their benefits.

Findings Regarding Question B (Macroeconomic Effects)

The impact of collective bargaining on macroeconomic performance can best be assessed through comparative studies where the performance of countries with (very) different bargaining systems is systematically compared. Most studies look at the economic performance of the OECD countries during the period from 1960 to 1998, and ask how the framework of collective bargaining affects a large number of macroeconomic performance indicators (such as unemployment and inflation) and labor market flexibility indicators (such as real wage flexibility) in an environment in which workers' rights can be taken as granted. The importance of collective bargaining as opposed to other ways of organizing contracting in the labor market can be measured by union density (the proportion of workers who are union members) and bargaining coverage (the proportion of the work force that is covered by a collective agreement). With respect to these indicators of collective bargaining, we find:

1. Union density per se has a very weak association, or perhaps no association, with economic performance indicators such as the unemployment rate, inflation, the employment rate, real compensation growth, labor supply, adjustment speed to wage shocks, real wage flexibility, and labor and total factor productivity. There is, however, one significant exception: union density correlates negatively with labor earnings inequality and wage dispersion.

2. Bargaining coverage tends to be associated with higher real wage growth (with no impact on productivity growth), lower employment rates, higher unemployment rates, and higher inflation. As with union density, bargaining coverage correlates negatively with labor earnings inequality and wage dispersion.

Collective bargaining is potentially a powerful means to facilitate *bargaining coordination;* that is, the extent of coordination between unions and employers' organizations in wage setting and other aspects of industrial relations (for example, working conditions, holidays and leave provisions and so on). Six different aspects of bargaining coordination can be identified: union centralization, union concentration, employer centralization, level of collective bargaining, informal coordination, and corporatism. Bargaining coordination is increasingly seen as an influential determinant of labor market and macroeconomic performance. For example, the Japanese system of wage setting is decentralized (firm-based) but coordinated in the sense that it follows company rules based on seniority (hence, they are transparent) rather than individual contracting. In this system, workers are not paid wages equal to their individual reservation wage (that is, the wage level below which the worker will not supply his or her labor), as would have been the case under individual contracting, but this difference does not adversely affect efficiency. The Netherlands and Germany also have coordinated systems through strong employer organizations, coordination among giant companies or across industries, and coordination among unions. In France the government provides coordination in the form of public services, utilities, and large nationalized industries. In Italy, there is informal employer coordination (via the big firms and regional employers' associations) and between some union confederations. Finally, Sweden has a centralized employers' organization as well as centralized union confederations. The comparative literature focuses on two hypothesizes about the relationship between bargaining coordination and economic performance:

> **Hypothesis 1.** Coordinated collective bargaining leads to better economic outcomes compared to semicoordinated collective bargaining, which, in turn, performs better than uncoordinated collective bargaining.

> **Hypothesis 2.** (The hump hypothesis) Semicoordinated collective bargaining leads to worse economic outcomes than both coordinated and uncoordinated collective bargaining.

The evidence suggests that bargaining coordination did have a beneficial impact on macroeconomic performance in the 1970s and 1980s, but the evidence is fragile and in the 1990s the impact seemed to disappear for most indicators. More specifically, we find:

3. Countries with highly coordinated collective bargaining tend to be associated with lower and less persistent unemployment, less earnings inequality and wage dispersion, and fewer and shorter strikes compared to countries with semicoordinated (for example, industry-level bargaining) or uncoordinated (for example, firm-level bargaining or individual contracting) collective bargaining. In terms of productivity growth and real wage flexibility, countries with highly coordinated collective bargaining tend to perform slightly better than countries with semicoordinated collective bargaining but may not perform differently than countries with uncoordinated collective bargaining. This lends some support to hypothesis 1, but only for the 1970s and 1980s. For most economic indicators, the differences disappear in the 1990s. Two exceptions are earnings inequality and wage dispersion. These indicators are comparatively low in countries with highly coordinated collective bargaining throughout the whole period.

4. Although countries with either uncoordinated or coordinated collective bargaining tend to be associated with lower and less persistent unemployment and higher productivity growth than semicoordinated collective bargaining during the period 1960 to 1990, the evidence in favor of the hump hypothesis is, in general, very weak, particularly for the 1990s.

5. In terms of inflation and the employment rate, there seems to be little difference between coordinated, semicoordinated, and uncoordinated collective bargaining.

These conclusions refer to one dimension of industrial relations and take other dimensions as given (either by controlling for them or by inappropriately ignoring them). This ignores the possibility of complementarities between union density/bargaining coverage and bargaining coordination. Such complementarities are important for the impact of collective bargaining on economic performance, and it can therefore be misleading to focus on one particular aspect in isolation. In particular, the following fact should be emphasized:

6. High union density and bargaining coverage do not contribute to poor unemployment performance so long as they are complemented by high bargaining coordination (particularly among employers).

Bargaining coordination is related to a number of different aspects of industrial relations, such as the centralization of collective bargaining, corporatism, informal coordination between employers or unions, and so on. As far as different types of coordination are concerned, the following points can be emphasized:

7. Informal coordination of wage bargaining (informal consultations between firms and/or unions or pattern bargaining) tends to mitigate the potential disadvantage (in terms of relative high unemployment) associated with semicoordinated (such as industry-level) wage bargaining, and can arise in countries with relatively low union density and bargaining coverage.
8. Coordination among employers tends to be more important in producing low unemployment than coordination among employees. This suggests that employers' organizations are more effective in controlling wage drift than union confederations.
9. Countries that have competing unions (multiunionism) and many different union confederations tend to perform worse (in terms of unemployment and inflation) than other countries.
10. The effects of coordination can be compromised or accentuated depending on the political orientation of the government. "Good" economic outcomes (in terms of economic growth) can arise either when strong, centralized unions are paired with a strong left-wing government or when weak, decentralized unions are paired with a right-wing government. A mismatch (weak unions paired with a strong left-wing government or strong unions paired with a right-wing government) can lead to poor economic outcomes.

This concludes the long list of specific macroeconomic findings. Although some patterns emerge, we feel that the evidence is too weak and fragile to warrant grand generalizations about the performance of specific labor market institutions. Instead, we want to stress that the relationship between collective bargaining and economic performance cannot be fully understood unless the general economic and political environment in which bargaining takes place is taken into account. One should therefore be careful not to infer that institutional forms that work well in one environment would also work well in other— often very different—environments. With this caveat in mind, the synthesis of the literature embodied in our list of findings can provide a useful starting point for more specific studies of labor market reform.

Labor Standards in a Global Environment

Assessing the economic effects of unions and collective bargaining is as important as it is difficult. A compelling argument is that workers should have a fair share of the benefits associated with economic growth, and when output falls, they should not be penalized for crises for which they are not responsible. The best way for governments and the international community to protect workers' interests and their families' welfare may be to promote economic efficiency and mechanisms that ensure a fair distribution of efficiency gains. The involvement of social partners may be a prerequisite for designing and implementing policies that reflect the preferences of society at large.

However, systems of coordination are neither easily replicable nor necessarily a panacea. The degree and kind of coordination at the labor market achieved in each case are country specific in terms of economic conditions and institutional and cultural characteristics. In most countries where coordination exists, it evolved gradually through piecemeal legislation over decades rather than as a massive policy intervention at a specific point in time. Although some policies may have created insiders and outsiders in the labor market, policies usually blend social concerns with the economic realities of the time. Of course, labor regulation introduced at a time when particular circumstances prevailed should be reconsidered when economic conditions change. Most of the countries with coordinated systems, especially in Europe, are in the process of changing, partly because of increasing exposure to external competition and partly because of the decline in manufacturing, where collective bargaining is more common than in white-collar sectors.

By extension, assessing the economic impact of core labor standards that relate to unions and collective bargaining is important for the international community, which is concerned with the effects of labor regulations on international trade. However, it is also important to know the economic effects of labor standards on individual countries. If freedom of association and the right to collective bargaining can be shown to have positive economic effects for the countries concerned, this will dissipate some of the heat in the "North-South" debate around the notion that when labor rights and labor standards differ between countries, such differences can give an "unfair" cost advantage in internationally traded goods to those countries that have lower standards.

Although some of the studies discussed in chapters 4 and 5 came from developing countries, most are from industrial countries. This raises the question of whether our conclusions are relevant to developing countries. One of the key findings of our survey is that the impact of unions and collective bargaining at both the microeconomic and the macroeconomic levels is context specific. The economic, legal, and political environment differs in many respects between the average industrial country and a typical developing or middle-income country. Most industrial countries have stable, liberal democracies and respect the two relevant labor standards in law and practice. This is not the case in many developing and middle-income countries. Nelson (1991) has pointed out that the type of political regime—ranging from democracy to dictatorship—significantly affects the way in which industrial relations develop. The same is true for the economic environment. The economic impact of unions in an environment of ill-designed labor and product markets in which rent seeking is profitable is very different from the economic impact of unions in a well-designed environment. To illustrate, in many developing countries, unions with close ties to the government have played an important role in sustaining import substitution policies. Krueger (1993: 86–87), for instance, writes:

> Because domestic private sector industry was protected by import prohibitions and licensing, most firms had considerable monopoly power. Labor unions, whose bargaining power had been strengthened by benevolent social guardian governments, were able to negotiate with private sector firms whose incentive to resist wage increases, given their monopoly position, was relatively weak. Although employment in the private sector industry grew very slowly, ..., those fortunate enough to have employment in the private sector industries became yet another group supporting economic policies [i.e. import substitution policies].

Moreover, in many developing countries, unions are concentrated in the formal sector, and in the public sector. The concentration of unions in the public sector makes them a powerful pressure group that can be a significant obstacle to structural reforms (see, for example, Freeman 1993a).

The relationship between social partners, however, need not always be a simple one. Some political scientists have made attempts to quantify the effects and have looked at the interaction between the strength of labor, party control, and economic outcomes. The argument here is that labor market parties, particularly unions, expect the government to deliver certain welfare goods and policies in exchange for wage moderation and peace in the labor market.

There can be many scenarios of such arrangements. For example, if unions are powerful and the government is left-wing, economic performance can be predicted to be "good." This is because the pursuit of welfare policies by left-wing parties is likely to lead to voluntary wage moderation. Moreover, if unions organize the majority of workers, they are less likely to engage in wasteful rent-seeking, since unionized workers would themselves bear most of the costs associated with these activities. Alternatively, if unions are politically weak and the government is right-wing, "good" economic performance can also be expected. This is because unions are restricted in their wage demands by competitive pressure from product markets that are left unregulated by the right-wing government.

In contrast, "bad" economic performance can result when there is a mismatch between the power of the labor movement and the political orientation of the government. If, for instance, a right-wing government coexists with powerful unions, the unions are unlikely to restrict their wage demands voluntarily because the government cannot be expected to deliver any welfare goods in return. Likewise, a left-wing government coexisting with weak unions cannot count on any voluntary wage moderation because individual unions are likely to pursue their own interests (wage pressure) without taking into account the economy-wide consequences of their actions. These scenarios of the political orientation of the government and the organizational power of unions ("the Garrett and Lange hypothesis of coherence") find some empirical support in a sample of OECD countries.

These considerations imply that one should be careful to draw policy conclusions for developing and middle-income countries directly from the OECD evidence. In particular, the discussion of bargaining coordination may be largely irrelevant at the current state for many developing and middle-income countries in which union density is low, unions are concentrated in the public sector, and the legal framework of industrial relations is only partially designed. Nevertheless, bargaining coordination can become increasingly an issue as industrial relations develop and unionization is extended to more sectors.

2

Economic Effects of
Labor Standards

The substantial cross-country variation in compliance with the two labor standards identified in table 1-1 begs the question: do these differences have any detectable impact on economic performance? The purpose of this chapter is to examine this question from a cross-country comparative perspective.

Labor Standards and Economic Performance

It is a difficult task to measure cross-country variation in labor standards and to disentangle their economic effects from other determinants of economic performance. One approach, which side steps the difficulties of obtaining comparable measures of labor standards across countries, is to identify countries that have undertaken major labor market reforms in the areas of freedom of association and the right to collective bargaining, and then to compare the performance of the economy *before* and *after* the reform. Using this approach, OECD (1996) has identified 17 countries that have undertaken significant labor market reforms over the past 20 years and has compared the average growth rate of GDP, manufacturing output, and exports in the five-year period before and the five-year period after the reforms. Table 2-1 summarizes the results of this exercise.

The evidence shows that on average, GDP grew at 3.8 percent per year before the improvement in labor standards and at 4.3 percent afterwards. Growth in manufacturing output increased by a smaller amount (from 3.4 to 3.6 percent). In contrast, export growth declined by 2.3 percentage points on average (from 6.6 to 4.3 percent). These averages mask considerable variation and can therefore be misleading. First, the averages hide huge differences in individual country experiences. For example, growth rates in Panama increased by as much as 8 to 10 percentage points

Table 2-1.   Economic Performance before and after an Improvement in Labor Standards

(average growth rates, percent)

Country	Reform year	GDP growth Before	After	Manufacturing output growth Before	After	Export growth Before	After
Argentina	1983	−0.2	1.0	−0.5	0	0.6	2.8
Brazil	1988	5.3	0.9	4.5	−2.2	9.5	4.8
Dominican Republic	1990	4.4	4.5	1.7	4.2	9.1	5.6
Ecuador	1979	7.1	1.3	11.6	2.1	0.4	2.3
Fiji	1987	9.8	5.8	4.2	−0.6	14.3	6.7
Guatemala	1992	4.1	4.1	—	—	5.6	8.6
Honduras	1990	3.0	3.3	4.0	3.8	1.9	1.8
Korea, Republic of	1987	10.7	8.6	15.7	8.3	15.6	6.9
Panama	1989	−0.5	10.5	−2.5	8.9	0.2	8.9
Peru	1990	−0.9	1.8	—	—	−3.8	−23.2
Philippines	1987	−1.3	4.0	−2.4	3.1	2.4	7.2
Suriname	1991	1.7	0.6	−3.2	−2.4	—	—
Taiwan (China)	1987	9.6	6.9	—	—	—	—
Thailand	1992	10.7	8.2	14.7	11.5	17.3	13.2
Turkey	1986	6.1	2.7	7.9	5.7	16.1	8.1
Uruguay	1985	−7.6	4.4	−5.4	3.7	2.7	6.8
Venezuela, Rep. Bolivariana de	1990	2.7	5.2	−3.3	4.5	6.8	3.6
Average		3.81	4.34	3.36	3.61	6.58	4.27

— Not available.

Source: OECD (1996, table 7).

after the reform, whereas export growth in Peru collapsed. Second, in most countries, economic performance actually deteriorated after the reform.

These results are crude, as growth performance depends on many other factors such as initial level of GDP, investment levels, political institutions and, in the shorter term, the growth rates in other countries. Hence, to isolate the (potential) impact of a reform, these factors have to be taken into account. Palley (1999) analyzes the relationship between GDP growth and improvements in labor standards in a multiple regression model. He estimates a pooled time-series/cross-country model using data for 15 of the countries included in table 2-1 five years before and five years after an improvement in labor standards took place.[1] He includes the following

---

1.   Taiwan (China) and Turkey are excluded.

control variables: lagged GDP growth, the average growth rate in the relevant region, the average growth in industrial countries, a linear time trend, a set of country dummy variables, and a dummy variable to capture the effect of the reform. He finds that improvements in labor standards have a positive and statistically significant effect on economic growth, with significance levels ranging from 0.01 to 0.12 depending on the precise specification of the estimated equation.

It is unclear, however, what can be learned about the impact of labor standards on economic growth from table 2-1 and these regressions. First, improvements in labor standards are typically an integral part of more comprehensive reforms that change the entire institutional structure of an economy. To the extent that this is the case, one cannot attribute the change (positive or negative) in economic performance to improvements in labor standards alone: the "reform dummy variable" used in the regressions picks up all changes in the political and economic environment. Second, while it is possible that changes in institutions and the legal structures can have an impact on economic performance in the short term, it normally takes a long time for such changes to spread throughout the economic system. Therefore, the impact is typically not observable until long after the reform has been initiated: the period under consideration is too short to allow us to make robust generalizations.

Freeman (1993a) takes a different approach. He provides a detailed investigation of the relationship between economic growth (and other economic performance indicators) and observance of core labor standards in six East Asian "success" countries.[2] Freeman (1993a: 45) concludes that the observance of core labor standards is neither an obstacle nor a necessity for economic growth and that "what is clear is that these countries as a group are not examples of developing countries that succeeded by avoiding labor interventions." This conclusion is supported by World Bank (1993), which argues that the suppression of unions in the Republic of Korea (prior to 1988) and wage repression in Singapore cannot be considered significant factors in the successful growth of these economies during the 1980s when compared to China, Hong Kong (China), and Taiwan (China).

In addition, Fields (1994) argues that Hong Kong (China), Singapore, the Republic of Korea, and Taiwan (China) have performed equally well during the considerable transformation of their economies over time despite significant differences in the industrial composition of their output and employment and despite huge differences in their labor markets. Thus, neither growth nor adjustment seems to relate singularly to

---

2.   China, Hong Kong (China), Malaysia, Singapore, the Republic of Korea, and Taiwan (China).

specific labor market characteristics or policies (Tzannatos 1996). In fact, the relationship between specific policy variables and economic growth is generally weak (Levine and Renelt 1992), and a comparative study of 31 industrial and developing countries estimates that labor market distortions cannot account for more than 10 percent of the cross-country variation in economic growth (Agarwala 1983).

Labor Standards and International Trade

The discussion in the previous chapter suggests that labor standards and international trade have figured prominently in the policy debate. On the one hand, low labor standards might be interpreted as social dumping and unfair trade practices. On the other hand, trade sanctions imposed with the aim of forcing low-standard countries to impose higher standards might be interpreted as protectionism. According to either of these arguments, compliance as well as non-compliance with core labor standards distorts international trade—compliance by favoring countries with high standards and noncompliance by favoring countries with low standards. A crucial question then is if there is any evidence of this actually happening. The OECD (1996) examines the interaction between freedom of association and the right to bargain collectively and various indicators of international trade using the country classification from table 1-1. Table 2-2 summarizes some of their conclusions.

Based on the evidence presented in table 2-2, there does not seem to be a systematic relationship between freedom of association and the right to collective bargaining and international trade, as measured by export market shares, revealed comparative advantage, foreign direct investments, and trade prices. However, the two labor standards appear to be associated positively with the success of trade reforms, although, as argued earlier, it is difficult to distinguish labor reforms from more general reforms in the political and economic spheres. Also, it is unclear if successful reform creates greater respect for workers' rights or if respect for workers' rights makes trade reforms successful. Finally, while examples of countries that have systematically suppressed labor rights in export processing zones (EPZs) do exist, the OECD concludes that selective suppression of workers' rights is not a general tendency (see also the review of EPZs in Kusago and Tzannatos 1998). Elliott and Freeman (2001) argue that EPZs can become a testing ground for demonstrating that trade and labor standards can reinforce one another in raising standards of living in poor countries.

Overall, it is clear that this important issue requires more research before it can be settled in a satisfactory way. Nevertheless, the controversy surrounding it seems unmatched by evidence that labor standards actually distort trade patterns in any significant way.

Table 2-2.   Relationship between Core Labor Standards and International Trade: Evidence from OECD and Non-OECD Countries

Trade indicator	Definition	Result
Trade performance	Growth in the share of a county's exports in total world trade (measured as total export, raw material export, or manufacturing export), 1980–90.	No correlation.
Revealed comparative advantage	Index for comparative advantage calculated for 71 sectors on the basis of foreign trade performance for these sectors.	No effect on the pattern of revealed comparative advantage. Comparative advantage is by and large determined by the abundance of factors of production and technology.
Trade prices	U.S. import prices of textiles from a group of other OECD and non-OECD countries.	No effect on border prices in the United States for similar imported textiles from different countries. Likewise, U.S. import of textiles from "high-standard" OECD countries has not been "crowded out" by imports from "low-standard" non-OECD countries.
Trade liberalization	The change in tariffs and quantitative trade restrictions, 1980–90.	Positive correlation with the trade liberalization.
Foreign direct investment (FDI)	OECD investment outflow to non-OECD countries, 1975–93.	Low labor standards not an important factor for investment decisions in OECD firms.
Export-processing zones (EPZs)	Firms in an area that offers privileges with regard to government policies.	Existence of evidence in only 6 of the 73 countries that have established EPZs of deliberate government attempts to restrict freedom to associate and the right to bargain collectively. The countries are Bangladesh, Jamaica, Pakistan, Panama, Sri Lanka, and Turkey.

Note: Labor standards refer to the freedom of association and the right to bargain collectively.

Source: OECD (1996 part II).

3

Collective Bargaining and Economic Performance—A Short Review of the Theory

Unions arise from the asymmetry in contracting between individual workers and employers, the concern for basic workers' rights, and different perceptions about the merits of employment relations governed by individual contracts and collective agreements. The desirability of unions depends on many factors, including (a) what unions do, (b) how collective bargaining is organized, and (c) the effectiveness of dispute resolution mechanisms. Freedom of association refers not only to the workers' right to form unions of their liking, but also to the right of employers to form employers' organizations. As with unions, the desirability of employers' organizations depends on what they do and the context in which they do it.

What Unions Do

Unions are engaged in many different activities. We make a distinction among three aspects of union behavior: monopoly, participatory, and rent-seeking behavior.

The Monopoly Cost of Unions

Traditionally, economists have focused on the social costs of unions, which arise when they secure favorable pay and work conditions for their members by sharing supernormal profits with firms (Booth 1995).[1]

---

1.   In a competitive market, the union is able to share in the quasi-rent to fixed capital in the short run, but in the long run, the unionized firm is forced to close down, and capital moves to a nonunionized sector where the return is higher.

Supernormal profits are typically associated with product market distortions and/or government regulation; thus, labor market and product market distortions are often viewed as complements. Unions can force firms to relinquish some of their profits only if they can monopolize labor supply.[2] This is because unions wield the strike threat: firms are willing to give up some of their profits to avoid industrial conflict. Competition from a large nonunionized labor market reduces the union's monopoly command over labor supply; if nonunion workers can readily replace union workers, the union's bargaining position is substantially weakened (Ulph and Ulph 1990).[3] According to this view, when unions succeed, they impose a number of costs on society, which we call the monopoly costs of unions. These costs are as follows:

- Firms will try to pass on the wage demands to consumers as higher prices. This increases the consumer price index and reduces the real (consumption) wage of all workers. It also increases the real price of intermediate inputs harming other producers. These effects are comparatively small if firms operate in a highly competitive (product) market environment.
- The wage markup increases the relative price of labor in the union sector. This induces a reallocation of labor to the nonunion sector as firms decide to lay off unionized workers (Rees 1963). This tends to reduce the nonunion wage and the welfare of nonunion members and leads to an output loss because workers are now being employed where their marginal productivity is lower than before (see Sapsford and Tzannatos 1993: 325–28). These effects are mitigated when unions and firms bargain over wages *and* employment (McDonald and Solow 1981), as employment increases rather than decreases in the unionized sector, reducing the negative spillover on nonunionized sectors.

---

2.   Some rents are capitalized in the value of the firm and so are not available for sharing. This effect can be illustrated as follows. Assume a monopoly situation is established as a result of an innovation. If the prospect for high profits is real, the inventor is likely to sell the right and make a large capital gain instantaneously. Thereafter, sales grow and the firm reverts to a public company. The monopoly power of the company is now reflected in the value of its shares, not in the rate of operating profit. It is the rate of return to the shares (in the form of dividends and capital gains) that is relevant for collective bargaining and this is determined competitively in the stock market. Hence, the firm's ability to provide high wages to its labor force has disappeared (Sapsford and Tzannatos 1993).

3.   The extent to which nonunion workers are a cost-effective substitute for union workers depends, among other things, on job security rules (the cost of hiring and firing), the availability of nonunion workers with the necessary skills, and institutional rules that allow the union to run a closed shop or otherwise link employment to union membership.

- Unionized firms share their profits with the union. This creates a hold-up problem that reduces investments in physical capital and R&D in unionized firms below the socially optimal level (Grout 1984).
- The more senior members, who typically have a disproportionate influence on union decisions, may institutionalize a seniority principle in relation to layoffs and other aspects of deployment, such as promotion, recall, and training. This can create insider/ outsider dynamics that can lead to persistently high levels of unemployment.

The discussion of the monopoly costs of unions is often based on the (implicit) assumption that the labor market in the absence of collective bargaining would be competitive. This assumption is overly optimistic, as the "removal" of unions may reveal market imperfections on the labor demand side in the form of monopsony.[4] Under these circumstances, the presence of unions may offer a second-best alternative to free competition and the countervailing influence of unions can result in outcomes closer to the competitive equilibrium than are offered by competition on the supply side of the labor market and monopsony on the demand side.[5]

In addition, it is by no means clear that a net welfare gain will follow if a unionized system of wage and employment determination is replaced by one in which contracts are negotiated between individual workers and their employers. This is because large transaction costs may be associated with numerous individual contract negotiations compared with those arising from setting a small number of "pattern bargains" by negotiation between unions and an employers' association. The outcome of these negotiations can subsequently be adopted throughout the economy much as in the centralized ("Scandinavian") labor market structure. The beneficial effect of centralized negotiations may be stronger in industrial economies where, given the inherently complex nature of the labor market, individual negotiation (at least in some sectors of the labor market) may be the only feasible alternative to a unionized system.

---

4.   Employers derive monopsony power from the fact that it is costly for a worker to leave the firm (because of the firm-specific human capital he or she has accumulated) and move to another city to get a new similar job.

5.   Many more imperfections are likely to coexist with unionism, some arising from motivational problems (efficiency wages) and others from insider power (Lindbeck and Snower 1989).

The Participatory Benefits of Unions

The "organizational view" of unions (also known as the second face of unions), associated with Freeman (1980a) and Freeman and Medoff (1979, 1984) among others, focuses on the economic benefits of unions. Unions facilitate worker-participation and worker-manager cooperation in the workplace. This can have efficiency-enhancing effects that jointly benefit workers and management. More specifically, the economic benefits, which we refer to as participatory benefits, arise from a number of sources, such as the following:

- Unions are institutions with a collective voice operating within internal labor markets. The union's role within this framework is to communicate worker preferences directly to the management, as well as to participate in the establishment of work rules and seniority provisions in the internal labor market. This changes the exit-voice tradeoff of workers by providing a channel through which they can express their grievances without having to leave the firm. This reduces turnover (voting with the feet), increases the incentive of employers to provide firm-specific training, and facilitates long-term working relationships that benefit all parties. In addition, unions can help to establish seniority provisions, which lessen the rivalry between experienced and inexperienced workers, among other things. This can increase the amount of informal, on-the-job training that the former is willing to provide to the latter (Freeman and Medoff 1979, 1984).

- Unions facilitate procedural arrangements and other agency services that help to reduce the likelihood of costly disputes about wage and employment conditions (Faith and Reid 1987).

- Unions help to enforce contracts between workers and management (Malcomson 1983). For example, if the market demand for a product is uncertain, workers may be reluctant to acquire firm-specific skills unless the firm can promise not to fire them if demand turns out to be low. Without a credible enforcement mechanism, the firm cannot make such a promise and workers acquire too few firm-specific skills. However, a union can help to enforce the promise if the firm prefers to honor the implicit agreement rather than to become embroiled in a strike.

- Unions can increase productivity by providing a channel through which labor can draw management's attention to changes in working methods or production techniques that may be beneficial to both parties. This channel also offers a mechanism by which the union can "shock" management into better practices (reduce X-inefficiency).[6]

Unions as Rent-seekers

Unions represent the special interests of their members in collective bargaining and in the political process. As pointed out by Pencavel (1995), unions generally promote policies that reduce competition in labor and product markets. This includes support for minimum wage legislation, trade protection, and so on. Unions support such policies if they increase the surplus available for sharing with the firm (the effect of less competitive product markets) or increase the union's bargaining power (less competition from nonunion labor markets).[7]

The political activities of unions (and other rent-seekers) generally involve three types of (static) costs. First, to the extent that the union is successful in getting government regulation, an economic distortion is created, and the resulting deadweight loss is a loss to society. Second, real resources are withdrawn from production to be used in rent-seeking. To the extent that the shadow price of these resources is positive, this constitutes a loss to society. Third, since the union's distributive success typically comes at the expense of nonunion workers and consumers, a union's political activities may be associated with large distributional costs. In addition to these static costs, rent-seeking can lead to dynamic costs. As Murphy, Schleifer, and Vishy (1993) argue, rent-seeking is particularly harmful to innovations and thus hampers economic growth. One argument is that innovators lack the political base needed to obtain the necessary licenses and permits and that innovative projects are typically long term and risky, which exposes them to expropriation. In short, where unions are part of a rent-seeking society, they impose a substantial political cost on society.

What Employers' Organizations Do

The members of an employers' organization are individual firms, typically within a particular industry. Each employers' organization may in

---

6.   X-inefficiency refers to a situation in which a firm's total costs are not minimized because the actual output from given inputs is less than the maximum feasible level.

7.   With regard to the regulation of the product market, the union and the firm have a common interest, and they may form a very effective distributional coalition (Rama 1997a; Rama and Tabellini 1998). On the other hand, they disagree with respect to labor market regulations such as job security legislation and minimum wages.

turn be a member of a national employers' organization. A firm may decide to join an employers' organization to improve its bargaining position with workers (possibly organized in a union). Firms derive their bargaining power from their ability to lock out workers. The cost of an industrial conflict from the point of view of an individual firm is larger than the cost to the industry as a whole. This is because an individual firm involved in a strike is likely to lose its market share to other firms in the industry that produce close substitutes. Accordingly, whereas each firm has an incentive to give in to wage demands (to avoid a local conflict), the industry as a whole has less incentive to do so, and by joining forces, it is easier for firms to resist wage demands from unions (see Dowrick 1993).

Employers' organizations can also help firms to avoid leap frogging. Leap frogging occurs when individual firms increase their wage rate to extract more effort from existing workers or to attract skilled workers from other firms (Layard, Nickell, and Jackman 1991). When all firms engage in this kind of behavior, the net result may well be that relative wages are unchanged but the level of all wages has increased substantially. A strong employers' organization that coordinates the behavior of individual firms can be helpful in internalizing this "efficiency wage externality" and preventing wage drift (as discussed above). In addition, employers' organizations play an important role in providing training (Soskice 1990). Since general training is a public good, firms are unlikely to provide much of it unless they are subject to external pressure. A strong employers' organization can provide training facilities for firms and can impose sanctions if a firm does not pay its share of the cost.

Organization of Collective Bargaining

The economic effects of unions depend on the way in which collective bargaining is organized. Of particular interest here is the degree of bargaining coordination. This section outlines four aspects of bargaining coordination from a theoretical perspective. The aspects are centralization, union concentration, informal coordination, and corporatism.[8]

Centralization of Collective Bargaining

Collective bargaining is centralized when the national union confederation and the national employers' organization can influence and control

---

8.   The relevant theoretical literature has been surveyed in great detail by Calmfors (1993), Henley and Tsakalotos (1993), Layard, Nickell, and Jackman (1991: chapter 2), and Moene and Wallerstein (1993a).

wage levels and patterns across the economy. The capacity to do so depends on many factors, including the level at which bargaining primarily takes place (the plant, the industry, or the national level) and whether or not the national organization(s) can control the behavior of their constituent organizations and avoid wage drift. Table 3-1 summarizes eight important aspects of bargaining centralization and evaluates the associated (static) costs and benefits.

The idea that centralization of collective bargaining can facilitate internalization of externalities has received particular attention in the literature and warrants a more detailed discussion than the one given in table 3-1. To fix ideas, imagine a society in which all workers are organized in unions. Then suppose that each firm negotiates with a company union. In this case, wage-setters bear only a small fraction of the total economic cost associated with a given increase in their real wage as they impose external costs on others. Table 3-2 defines six such externalities in more detail. Because of these externalities, the negotiated wage is "too" high and the result is, other things being equal, "too" little total employment. By centralizing the bargaining process to the industry or national level, wage-setters are forced to bear a larger share of the cost of their actions, as more (and ultimately all) workers are included in the bargaining coalition. This creates incentives in favor of wage restraint, which, again other things being equal, leads to more total employment.

As pointed out by Calmfors and Driffill (1988), this argument ignores the fact that the competitive pressure from product markets and the moderating effect it has on wage demands change systematically with the level of centralization. For example, consider what happens when a union demands (and gets) a high nominal wage. To avoid an increase in the product real wage, firms pass on the cost to consumers as higher prices. From the union's point of view, not only does this reduce the consumption real wage but it has the unpleasant side effect of reducing the demand for the goods produced by the host firm, endangering the jobs of union members. Anticipating this outcome, the union moderates its wage demand. At the firm level, the competitive pressure from other firms in the same industry (producing close substitutes) provides a strong incentive to moderate demands. At the national level, the federation of unions bears the full cost of its actions, social partnerships become possible, and unions and employers' organizations are sufficiently encompassing to make rent-seeking unprofitable (Olson 1982; Heitger 1987). At the industry level, neither of these effects produces much wage moderation. On the contrary, firms in an industry can pass on a substantial portion of the wage demands to consumers at a relatively low employment cost. In addition, industry-based unions often form effective lobbying groups that seek distributive favors from the government at the expense of society at large.

Table 3-1. The Economic Costs and Benefits of the Centralization of Collective Bargaining

Issue	Benefit	Cost
1. *Internalization of externalities:* Unions and firms acting independently of the rest of the market (decentralization) can have unintended negative effects (externalities) on the rest of the economy (for example, higher wages can be passed on to consumers in the form of higher prices, higher inflation, and an increase in unemployment).	Centralization increases the size of the bargaining coalition, thereby internalizing negative externalities. The effect is larger, the more workers are unionized.	
2. *Competitive pressure:* Competition in product markets disciplines unions and firms, and this effect is strongest at a decentralized level (more competition reduces the ability to pass wage increases on to consumers as higher prices).		As bargaining becomes more centralized, competitive pressure is reduced because firms acting in unison are less likely to lose their market share (product demand is more inelastic at the industry level than at the firm level). This increases wage pressure and leads to higher unemployment. This effect is less important in an open economy.
3. *Wage compression:* Under centralized collective bargaining, solidarity/egalitarian wage goals are easier to achieve, and firm-specific conditions are less likely to enter the wage contracts. This tends to reduce wage dispersion.	Although wage compression can force less efficient firms out of the market (to the extent that low wages move upward), it can encourage the entry of new and more efficient firms: the net effect can, under certain conditions, increase output. Again, under certain assumptions, wage compression can act as a form of social insurance.	A reduction in wage dispersion leads to an economic misallocation of resources and lower output.
4. *Areas of bargaining:* Some issues can only be subject to collective bargaining at certain levels of centralization or above (training, health and safety, and so on).	For example, general training of workers is more likely to be part of centralized collective bargaining because it has the characteristics of a public good. Subsequently, training can lead to higher economy-wide labor productivity and overall economic growth.	Efficient bargaining (over employment and wages) is feasible only under decentralized bargaining. Workplace cooperation and other participatory activities between unions and firms decrease under centralized bargaining.

(table continues on following page)

Table 3-1 continued

Issue	Benefit	Cost
5. *Hold-up problems*: Firms undertake investment decisions today that affect future profits. If workers, via collective bargaining, can get a share of these profits without contributing to the costs, firms would underinvest.	The hold-up problem is reduced under centralized bargaining because an individual firm cannot affect the outcome of collective bargaining by its pre-bargaining investment decisions. This encourages firms to invest more.	
6. *Insider-induced hysteresis*: Only the group of insiders (for example, union members and employed workers) counts in wage bargaining. When the number of insiders is reduced (for example, after layoffs in a recession), they can push for higher wages in the next bargaining round and cause unemployment to remain persistently high (insider-induced hysteresis).	Under centralized bargaining, more workers can be perceived to be insiders (including the unemployed) to the extent that unions are concerned about aggregate unemployment.	
7. *Strikes*: Imperfect information can lead to more strikes.	Centralization increases the level of information about demand conditions, reducing the likelihood of strikes, especially wild-cat strikes.	Centralization increases the risk of a general strike.
8. *Bargaining power*: The relative bargaining power of workers and employers depends on the "fall-back" option of the two parties (what they will get if an agreement is not reached).	Centralization can reduce wage pressure by increasing employers' bargaining power because if all firms lock out workers during an industrial conflict, workers will have fewer alternative job opportunities.	Centralization can increase wage pressure if unions derive their bargaining power from the monopoly command over labor supply. It is easier for a single firm than for an entire industry or nation to replace workers in the event of a strike.

Source: Besides the surveys by Calmfors (1993), Henley and Tsakalotos (1993), Layard, Nickell, and Jackman (1991: chapter 2), and Moene and Wallerstein (1993a), the following references are relevant: (1) and (2) Calmfors and Driffill (1988); (3) Agell and Lommerud (1992), Harcourt (1997), Moene and Wallerstein (1993b, 1993c), and Agell (1998); (4) Soskice (1990); (5) Grout (1984); (6) Blanchard and Summers (1986); and (7) Kennan (1986).

31

Table 3-2.   Five Important Externalities Associated with Decentralized Wage-Setting

Externality	Definition
Input price	Decentralized wage gains are passed on as higher product prices, thus increasing the real cost of inputs for other firms.
Fiscal	Decentralized wage gains lead to unemployment. The cost in terms of unemployment benefits is borne by all taxpayers, not just those involved in wage-setting.
Unemployment	Decentralized wage gains increase overall unemployment, making it more difficult for all unemployed workers to find a new job.
Envy	Decentralized wage gains create envy among other workers.
Consumer price	Decentralized wage gains are passed on as higher product prices, thus lowering the real wage of all workers.
Efficiency wage	At the decentralized level, firms have an incentive to try to raise the relative wage of their workers to increase their motivation.

Source: Calmfors (1993: 5–6).

It follows from this discussion that the relationship between economic performance and centralization of collective bargaining can be nonlinear (U- or hump-shaped): relatively good performance for decentralized and centralized systems, but relatively poor performance for systems based on industry-level bargaining (Calmfors and Driffill 1988). It should be noted, however, that this prediction is sensitive to many of the underlying assumptions. For example, Rama (1994) shows that the nonlinear relationship tends to disappear in an open economy as competitive pressure becomes more intense at all levels of bargaining. It is also clear that centralization will not help to internalize external costs unless most workers are union members or have their pay and work conditions determined by collective agreements. More critical, perhaps, is the fact that the analysis takes a static view of the economy. Arguably, one of the key advantages of a centralized bargaining system is that it enables a coordinated and fast response to changing economic conditions.

A further complication arises in multi-bargaining systems where wage drift can be a problem whenever the national organizations cannot perfectly control the behavior of their constituencies. The term "wage drift" refers to wage increases negotiated at the firm level in addition to those specified in the agreement between the national organizations. The success of firm-level unions in obtaining wage drift depends on their bargaining power relative to that of (the local) management. Although management in general is interested in low wages, they may nevertheless be willing to accept local wage increases for efficiency wage reasons. Accordingly, not only does the union confederation have to control the behavior of its constituency, but the national employers' organization also has to make sure that its members stay in line. This is typically done by requiring that all local agreements be approved by the national employers' organization. Moreover, to reduce militancy at the firm level, strikes and lockouts may be banned after an agreement has been signed by the two national organizations (a peace clause). As noted by Calmfors (1993) and others, this is not likely to reduce wage drift significantly because unions can use informal sanctions (such as work-to-the-rule and go-slow actions) to improve their bargaining position. Therefore, in practice, it is difficult to prevent wage drift. To avoid its adverse impact, however, national organizations can try to internalize the expected wage drift in the agreements that they reach at the national level.

Union Concentration

The term "union concentration" is used to describe the horizontal organization of unions at a given level of centralization. Two characteristics of the horizontal organization of unions are normally stressed. These are multiunionism versus single-unionism and open versus closed unions. Multiunionism refers to a situation in which many competing unions offer to represent the same worker. An example of a country with multiunionism is Belgium where workers can choose from among a socialist, liberal, or Christian union or the United Kingdom where unions commonly compete at the plant level. In contrast, Denmark is characterized by single-unionism in the sense that the social-democratic labor movement almost has a monopoly on organizing workers. A closed union restricts membership to workers of a particular craft, profession, or job. The United Kingdom and the Scandinavian countries are examples of countries where closed unions are prevalent. In contrast, an open union allows workers with different levels of education and from different trades to be members. Examples of open unions include company and industry unions (which are open to all employees of the relevant company or industry), as in Japan and Germany. We say that an industrial relations system based on multiunionism and closed unions is less concentrated than one based on single-unionism and open unions.

To understand why the distinction between open and closed unions is important, imagine a firm whose work force of blue- and white-collar workers is organized in two closed unions. Each of these unions bargains separately with management over wages and work conditions for its particular constituency. The agreement between management and the firm's blue-collar workers affects the employment opportunities of the white-collar workers and vice versa. This is because the firm adjusts its employment mix in response to the change in the relative wage rate between the two types of workers. In other words, each of the two closed unions imposes an externality on the workers of the other union. This externality is internalized if all workers in the firm join one (open) union. The impact on wage demands depends on whether blue- and white-collar workers are substitutes or complements in production. Suppose that they are substitutes. Under a closed union structure where the two groups bargain separately, blue-collar workers are pleased if the white-collar union is successful in getting a pay raise and vice versa. This is because the pay raise for blue-collar workers increases the demand for white-collar workers as the firm substitutes toward the less expensive alternative. Under an open union structure, the fact that the two groups of workers bargain together ensures that the (positive) wage externality is internalized. Consequently, an open union pushes harder for wage increases than the two closed unions together. As a result, overall employment is likely to be lower. If, on the other hand, white- and blue-collar workers are complements in production, the externality associated with a closed union structure is negative. Accordingly, a single open union reduces wage pressure, and overall employment is likely to be higher.

To see why the distinction between single- and multiunionism is important, consider the costs and benefits of multiunionism. First, when unions compete to organize the same pool of workers, they are likely to end up organizing workers who are substitutes in production. As discussed above, the (positive) wage externality associated with separate bargaining tends to produce real wage moderation and high employment. On the other hand, if the competing unions need to prove their ability to raise wages to attract members, the outcome of competition between unions may be less rather than more employment. Second, workers are likely to have different preferences regarding the services provided by the union, such as the tradeoff between wage gains and employment and the nature of the political activities that the union engages in. Multiunionism allows workers to self-select into the union that best fits their preferences. Third, the preferences of the union leaders and those of the ordinary members may be different. For instance, while the members may want wage gains and job security, the leadership wants to maximize its power position. Because of asymmetric information, a moral hazard problem may arise. Under multiunionism, the ordinary members can vote with their feet. This may help to control this moral hazard problem and improve welfare. Fourth, the fact that each firm has to deal with more than one union may lead to excessive bargaining costs.

Informal Coordination

Bargaining coordination need not be embodied in the formal institutional framework of collective bargaining. It can be informal. Informal coordination typically takes two forms. The first form is *internal* coordination among employers and/or employees. On the employers' side, this involves coordination between industry-based employers' organizations or individual firms. This plays an important role in Austria, Japan, and Switzerland (Soskice 1990; OECD 1994). On the employees' side, internal coordination typically involves coordination between company- and industry-based unions. The second form of informal coordination is *pattern bargaining*. Here, a dominant industry or company enters a collective agreement that is followed by other firms and industries. This has been important in Germany, where the metal industry has traditionally acted as the leader. It is clear that informal coordination mechanisms are more fragile than those embodied in the formal institutions and are more likely to break down in times of rapid economic and social change or instability, when they are most needed.

Corporatism

The term corporatism is used to describe situations in which the economic and political activities of unions and employers' organizations take place within a well-defined framework of social partnership between workers, capitalists, and government (see, for example, Aidt 1997; Bruno and Sacks 1985; Cameron 1984; Henley and Tsakalotos 1993; Lehmbruch 1984; Tarantelli 1986). Within this framework, labor market parties, in particular unions, expect the government to deliver certain welfare goods and policies in exchange for wage restraint (Lange and Garrett 1985). In addition, social partnership can create social consensus and reduce the level of conflict in the labor market. It reduces the cost of implementing economic reforms when they are needed and helps mitigate coordination failures arising when, in the face of changing economic conditions, the economy needs to move from one equilibrium to another. It also facilitates income policy, economy-wide agreements on wages and weekly hours, health and safety standards, and so on. All these aspects help to bring about "good" economic outcomes. It is, however, important to notice that social partnerships have a tendency to break apart. The point is simple: unions, employers' organizations, and individual firms have an incentive to break away from their respective confederations to act on their own.

Dispute Resolution

The breakdown of negotiations between individual workers and their employers can take various forms, ranging from poor relations in the workplace (with potential costs including decreased levels of labor productivity through poor morale) to labor turnover (the "exit" option, with the potential loss to the employer of previously made investments in the workers' human capital). At the level of collective contracting, the stakes are arguably much higher for both workers (and their unions) and employers, with the ultimate cost of a negotiation breakdown being lost incomes for the workers and lost profits for employers. Given the potentially high level of these costs to both contracting parties, it is likely that workers and employers have a strong incentive to achieve a solution in preference to conflict. Like all good threats, the employer's threat of a lockout and the union's threat of a strike are best if they ensure that an agreement is reached before they are implemented.

In reality, collective bargaining does sometimes break down, and production, labor earnings, and profits are lost. It is certainly not safe to assume that the total of such costs is greater under the collective bargaining system than under the individual contracting system. We simply do not know whether these costs to society are greater or less than those that would arise from a breakdown in individual employer-employee pay negotiations. Indeed, given economies of scale in the production and dissemination of information, there are grounds for believing that the collective system, through its ability to resolve disputes, may be a less costly option from a social point of view than individual contracting.

There is a strong presumption that when disputes do occur under collective bargaining, it is because of asymmetries in the information possessed by the involved parties (Hicks 1932). A common example is when the trade union "misjudges" the maximum wage that the employer is willing or able to pay. Under such circumstances, the existence of regulation can prove decisive in resolving disputes through its information-gathering and -disseminating roles.

To understand the process, it is important to recognize the distinction between the union proper (sometimes called the official union) and its rank and file membership. Under this tripartite framework, the official union (often as a well-informed professional body) acts as an intermediary between the union membership and the employer. As such, its role is to reconcile the aspirations of the former against what it judges (on the basis of its more complete knowledge of the overall situation than that possessed by the union membership) that the employer would agree to pay. This reconciliation between worker aspirations and labor market realities may be achieved without either party having to resort to its no-trade sanction. However, should negotiations break down and a dispute occur, the role of the official union as a purveyor of information continues, with information being disseminated in both directions regarding concessions acceptable to each party and any new information that may materialize as the dispute progresses. This transmission of information continues until demands fall into balance with offers, at which time a settlement is achieved.

Viewing a union as an information-gathering and -disseminating body suggests that governments might want to adopt policies that increase the efficacy with which unions fill this role. The introduction of so-called cooling-off periods, during which all parties take time to assess the situation fully before implementing no-trade strategies, is one example. Other such policies might require that the employer (generally seen as the party in possession of more complete information) divulge to the union and its members certain types of information, perhaps in a standard form, to minimize the possibility that disputes will arise because workers incorrectly estimate the employer's ability to pay.

Some conflict is inevitable when wages and other employment conditions are set by negotiation (either collective or individual), rather than by the invisible hand of the market. Recognizing this fact, there are grounds for believing that a centralized, union-based system of wage bargaining may be less costly to society than an individually based negotiating system in terms of both total transaction costs and dispute costs. We have also seen that unions have a role in resolving disputes if they should occur.

Unions: Net Costs or Net Benefits?

We can summarize the theoretical discussion of the costs and benefits of unions using the following simple equation:

Net benefit of unions = participatory and dispute resolution benefits - monopoly costs - rent-seeking costs.

Alternatively, one can talk of cost and rewrite this equation as

Net cost of unions = monopoly costs + rent-seeking costs - participatory and dispute resolution benefits.

From a theoretical perspective, the net benefit/cost of unions is ambiguous and dependent on the relative size of the three components. These in turn depend significantly on the economic, political, and organizational environment in which collective bargaining takes place. The economic environment affects both the monopoly costs and the participatory benefits. The political environment determines the rent-seeking activities of unions. The organizational environment (bargaining coordination, social partnership, and dispute resolution) affects all three components. Thus, judging the contribution of unions and collective bargaining more generally to the achievement of economic and social outcomes is, at the end of the day, an empirical question.

4

Empirical Evidence from Microeconomic Studies

In this chapter, we examine a large body of empirical evidence about the economic effects of unions derived from microeconomic data on individual workers and establishments. Most of the evidence comes from the United States and the United Kingdom but some evidence is available from other industrial countries and from some developing countries. The chapter is organized as follows. First, we present evidence on the union/nonunion wage markup. This is by far the most well-researched aspect of union behavior, with more than 200 studies having been conducted in the United States alone. We examine cross-country differences in the average wage markup, as well as variations in the wage markup across skills, gender, occupation, and ethnicity along with the underlying economic and institutional environment. We then examine the effect of unions on other economic variables such as employment growth, hours worked, productivity, job mobility, the implementation of new technology, physical investments, spending on R&D, training of workers, profitability, fringe benefits, mode of pay, and pension schemes. Finally, we discuss and evaluate the costs and benefits of unions and relate the net cost of unions to the underlying economic and institutional environment.

The Wage Markup in Different Countries

The union/nonunion wage markup (the "wage markup") is defined as the difference between the average (nominal) wage of unionized and nonunionized workers with similar individual and workplace characteristics divided by the average wage of a nonunionized worker.[1] The markup

---

1.   In principle, we are interested in comparing the union wage with the wage that would have prevailed in the absence of unions (this is called the "wage gain"). However, the wage gain is unobservable, and the literature focuses on the wage markup.

can be estimated in different ways. First, it can be estimated as a *membership markup*. The membership markup is based on information about an individual's union status and calculates the difference in wages between individual unionized and nonunionized workers. Second, it can be estimated as a *recognition markup*. Here workers are being categorized according to whether or not their pay is determined by a collective agreement between a recognized union and a firm. In the latter case, individual union membership is not crucial. What matters is whether the workers' pay is determined by a collective agreement. The distinction between the membership and the recognition markup is important when not all the workers whose wages are determined by a collective agreement are union members. For example, when many workers are covered by collective agreements although they are not members of a union (such as in the United Kingdom and Germany), estimates based on the membership markup underestimate the "true" markup, and it is preferable to use the recognition markup to measure the impact of unions on wages.

The estimation of the wage markup can be based on data on the wages of individual workers or average sectorwide or occupational wage rates (for example, average wages in different industries or broad sectors, such as manufacturing versus services or manual versus nonmanual workers). As it is generally agreed that the markup calculated using sectorwide data is biased upwards, we focus on studies that have used individual cross-sectional data (Lewis 1986; Booth 1995). One estimation approach is to analyze *separately* how wages are determined for unionized and nonunionized workers. The markup can then be estimated as the difference that arises from differences in the coefficients of the two regressions weighted with the average characteristics of workers in the sample. Another estimation approach is to pool all observations for individual workers and run a regression of wages on key characteristics plus an additional (dummy) variable indicating union membership. Historically, both approaches have been used, but more recent estimates are predominantly based on the former approach. This is because the latter approach implicitly assumes that there is a uniform wage determination process for unionized and nonunionized workers—an assumption that is not necessarily justified in practice.

A major econometric problem involved in estimating the wage markup is to control for all other factors besides unionization that affect wages. These factors have typically been proxied by variables such as education, work experience, gender, family status, hours worked, firm size, industry, occupation, and so on. However, some of these variables may be highly correlated with union status. For example, the fact that a given unionized worker works longer hours than a given nonunionized worker may be the result of union negotiated overtime, or, in another example, working in a particular industry may be a critical factor for belonging to a union (such as in the mining sector). In addition, Duncan and Stafford (1980) point out that part of the observed difference between the wages of unionized and nonunionized workers is compensation for different work conditions. They hypothesize that unions develop most often in situations where collective decisions must be made on work conditions that affect all workers and where work conditions cannot be tailored to individual needs. Since these are precisely the kinds of situations in which (unionized) workers need to be compensated for being in a work environment that is worse than the environment in which nonunionized workers operate, the higher earnings of union members may reflect, in part, compensating wage differentials rather than rents. Another problem is union-status selectivity. This problem arises because the union-status selection process is not random. For example, workers with high productivity may decide not to join a union or decide to work in the nonunion sector because they hope to get a higher wage than the wage that was collectively agreed on. This phenomenon gives rise to selectivity bias and reduces the reliability of the estimated markup.[2] Bearing these remarks in mind, we present below a summary of country-specific studies on the wage markup as well as cross-country comparisons.[3]

Country-Specific Studies

In all countries where the wage markup has been estimated, it has been found to be nonnegative. There are, however, significant cross-country variations as well as variations of estimates within countries. There is also some evidence, albeit weak, that the wage markup is, on average, lower in high-income countries than in low- and middle-income ones. More specifically, table 4-1 presents summary estimates of the wage markup for six high-income economies (Australia, Canada, Japan, the United Kingdom, the United States, and West Germany), four middle-income economies (Malaysia, Mexico, South Africa, and the Republic of Korea), and one low-income economy (Ghana).

---

2.   One way to deal with the union-status selectivity problem is to estimate the wage equation and a union-status selection equation simultaneously. Another is to use a panel data set that contains a time-series of cross-sections for the same set of workers. This makes it possible to control for unobserved heterogeneity. For example, if unobserved characteristics of workers stay constant over time, they can be taken into account by comparing the wage of each worker at one date with his or her wage at a later date. One problem with this solution is that identification is based on workers who change their status, and that is a relatively infrequent event. Lewis (1986) is unable to determine the likely size and direction of the selectivity bias.

3.   Extensive discussion on methodological issues on the estimation of the wage markup can be found in Booth (1995), Lewis (1986), Pencavel (1991), and Sapsford and Tzannatos (1993).

Table 4-1. Union/Nonunion Wage Markup for Selected Countries

Country	Period/Year	Wage markup (percent)
High-income economies		
Australia	1984–87	7–17
Canada	1969–94	10–25
Japan		5
United Kingdom	1969–95	10
United States	1963–95	15
West Germany	1985–87	0–6
Middle-income economies		
Korea, Republic of	1988	2–4
Malaysia	1988	15–20
Mexico	1989	10
South Africa	1993–95	10–24
Low-income economies		
Ghana	1992–94	21–28

Note: Figures in the table indicate the range of the estimated *average* markup for each country. When a single figure is reported, it refers to a single study except in the case of the United Kingdom and the United States where the reported figures are "summary-best-guesses" (Lewis 1986; Booth 1995). For studies based on cross sectional U.S. data, the range of the markup is 14 to 17 percent. For studies based on panel U.S. data, the range is 7 to 10 percent (Lewis 1986). The corresponding range for the United Kingdom is 3 to 19 percent.

Source: **Australia:** Christie (1992) (16 to 17 percent in 1984), Kornfeld (1993) (7 to 10 percent in 1984-87), Mulvey (1986) (7 percent for women and 10 percent for men in 1982); **Canada:** Grant, Sivindinshyn, and Vanderkamp (1987) (12 to 14 percent in 1969 and 13 to 14 percent in 1970), Green (1991) (15 percent in 1986); Gunderson (1982) (10 to 20 percent); Gunderson, Ponak, and Taras (2000) (10 to 25 percent), MacDonald (1983), MacDonald and Evans (1981), Robinson and Tomes (1984), Simpson (1985) (11 percent in 1974); **Japan:** Nakumura, Sato, and Kamiya (1988); **Korea, Republic of:** Kim (1993), Park (1991); **United Kingdom:** Booth (1995), Pencavel (1991), Sapsford and Tzannatos (1993); **United States:** Lewis (1986, 1990); **West Germany:** Schmidt (1995), Schmidt and Zimmermann (1991), Wagner (1991); **Malaysia:** Standing (1992); **Mexico:** Panagides and Patrinos (1994); **South Africa:** Dabalen (1998), Moll (1993); **Ghana:** Teal (1996).

The most reliable picture comes from the United States and the United Kingdom by virtue of the many studies that have been carried out and the broad consistency of the results. The U.S. wage markup has been estimated in more than 200 studies. While the estimates range from 12 to 22 percent, there is consensus that the *average* markup is approximately 15 percent (Blanchflower 1996a, 1997; Booth 1995; Lewis, 1986). Filer, Hamermesh, and Rees (1996: 499), however, argue that the wage markup significantly overestimates the wage gain and that the true impact of unions on wages in the United States is only between 8 and 12 percent. In the United Kingdom, more than 20 studies have estimated the markup to be in the range of

3 to 19 percent. Booth (1995: chapter 6) argues that the markup is approximately 10 percent on average (see also Blanchflower 1997).

The evidence is sparser for other industrialized economies, but some generalizations are possible. The wage markup for Australia has been estimated to vary between 7 and 17 percent. Similarly, the Canadian wage markup has been estimated to be in the range of 10 to 25 percent, although most estimates seem to fall in the 10 to 15 percent range. Gunderson, Ponak, and Taras (2000) find that the Canadian wage markup was increasing during the 1970s but has been decreasing ever since, reaching a low of 10 percent in the beginning of the 1990s. In (West) Germany, where most unions are industry unions and work and pay conditions contained in collective agreements are largely extended to nonunionized workers, the wage markup is found to be small, especially for male workers. Similarly, a study on Japan has found a small average wage markup of about 5 percent. As in (West) Germany, the average estimate hides large gender differences (see below).

The evidence is even more limited for low- and middle-income economies. In the Republic of Korea, Park (1991) estimates the markup for male workers in manufacturing industries to be below 4 percent in 1988. The union membership wage markup in South Africa has been estimated in three studies. Moll (1993) estimates the markup to be around 24 percent for black blue-collar workers. Dabalen (1998) finds that the mean wage markup for workers is about 19 percent. However, a recent study by Butcher and Rouse (2001) argues that these figures overestimate the wage markup. In any case, these estimates hide interesting variations between workers with different skills and with different racial characteristics. We return to this fact below when we discuss the differences in the markup by ethnic group and the markup to workers with different skills. Standing (1992) estimates the wage markup for Malaysia to be in the range of 15 to 20 percent depending on the type of union involved. These effects are somewhat larger than in most industrial countries. Standing attributes this high markup to the fact that Malaysian nonunionized workers can, in the absence of minimum wage legislation, be vulnerable to very low wages. He concludes that the markup can reasonably be in the estimated range even though the political and economic environment in Malaysia is difficult for unions.

For Mexico, Panagides and Patrinos (1994) find a 10 percent membership wage markup after having controlled for a large number of income-generating characteristics in a cross-sectional sample of unionized and nonunionized nonagricultural workers in 1989. They attribute the relative low wage markup to the fact that the 1980s were a particularly difficult time for unions in Mexico because of a recession coupled with government austerity measures. It is unclear, however, if this explains the result. First, recession and austerity measures should affect unionized and nonunionized sectors alike. Second, one could argue that unions would be in a better position than nonunionized workers to resist downward pressure on wages, thereby increasing the wage markup during a recession.

For Ghana, Teal (1996), using three surveys of manufacturing firms in 1992, 1993, and 1994, finds that the wage markup varies between 21 and 28 percent.[4] Again, these estimates are significantly higher than those in industrial countries. Teal notes that his cross-section estimates can be biased because of omitted variables (such as unobserved productivity differences) that are correlated with earnings and the union status of the firms. His panel estimates, however, suggest that the selectivity bias may not be a serious problem.

Comparative Studies

Some studies have estimated the membership wage markup in a cross-country context (Blanchflower 1996b; Blanchflower and Freeman 1992; Blanchflower and Oswald 1994). These studies use comparable individual worker data for the period 1985 to 1993 to estimate hourly earnings equations using similar control variables (such as age, gender, years of schooling, hours worked, and so on). This makes it possible to compare the estimates for different countries directly. Unfortunately, there is no information on industry and establishment size for most countries (with the notable exceptions of the United States and the United Kingdom). These variables are likely to be positively correlated with union status and wage rates. For example, large establishments tend to pay higher wages and have more unionized workers than small establishments. As a consequence, the estimates presented in table 4-2 are likely to overstate the wage markup. On the other hand, the estimates refer to a membership wage markup. As discussed above, in countries such as Austria and Germany where almost all workers, unionized or not, are covered by collective agreements, such estimates tend to understate the true effect of unions on wages.

As table 4-2 indicates, the markup is positive in all countries, but not significantly so in Canada, Israel, the Netherlands, Spain, and Switzerland.[5] On the other hand, the estimates for Ireland and Japan are extremely

---

4.   Contrary to most of the other studies reviewed, Teal (1996) uses a cross-section of firm-level average wages rather than a cross-section (or panel) of worker wages to estimate the markup. Therefore, the markup refers to the union status of the firm and not to an individual's membership in a union.

5.   The estimates for Israel, Spain, and Switzerland are, however, based on only a few hundred observations.

**Table 4-2.   Union/Nonunion Wage Markup and Characteristics of
Collective Bargaining Systems for 15 Countries**

Country	Centralization/ coordination, 1990 (1)	Union density, 1990 (percent) (2)	Bargaining coverage, 1990 (percent) (3)	Change in union density 1970–93 (4)	Wage markup, 1985–93 (percent) (5)
Australia	1	41	80	B	9.2
Austria	1	46	98	A	14.6
Canada	3	36	38	C	4.8*
Germany	1	33	83	C	3.4
Ireland	—	52	—	B	30.5
Israel	—	—	—	—	7.0*
Italy	3	39	23	C	7.2
Japan	2	25	71	A	47.8
Netherlands	2	26	67	C	3.7*
New Zealand	3	45	75	B	8.4
Norway	1	56	79	C	7.7
Spain	2	13	76	D	0.3*
Switzerland	2	27	53	B	0.8*
United Kingdom	3	39	47	B	14.7
United States	3	16	18	A	23.3

— Not available.

Note: Column 1: The numbers indicate the following: 1. highly centralized/coordinated wage bargaining system; 2. semicentralized/coordinated wage bargaining system; 3. decentralized/uncoordinated wage bargaining system (OECD 1997: table 3.3).

Column 2: Union density is the proportion of all wage- and salary-earners that is unionized (OECD 1997: table 3.3).

Column 3: Bargaining coverage is the number of workers covered by collective agreements as a percentage of all wage- and salary-earners (OECD 1997: table 3.3).

Column 4: The letters indicate the following: A. declining union density over the period 1970–93; B. increasing union density in the 1970s but declining thereafter; C. declining density in the 1980s, but stabilizing in the 1990s; D. a sharp increase in union density from 1970 to 1993 (Blanchflower 1996b: table 2).

Column 5: An asterisk (*) indicates that the estimate is not significantly different from zero (Blanchflower 1996b).

Source: Blanchflower (1996b); OECD (1997).

high (31 percent and 48 percent, respectively), perhaps reflecting the lack of control for industry and establishment size. Compare, for example, the estimate for Japan in table 4-1 (5 percent) with the estimate in table 4-2 (48 percent). In addition, the estimates for the United States and the United Kingdom are about 50 percent higher than the widely accepted average estimates of 15 percent and 10 percent, respectively, reported in table 4-1.

This gives some idea of the extent to which the estimates from the other countries may be exaggerating the true impact of unions. We notice that the wage markup in the United States is higher than the markup in all the other OECD countries except Ireland and Japan. The markup in Austria and the United Kingdom is also high by international standards, whereas the markup in other European countries and Australia is more modest.

Can this pattern be attributed to institutional differences among the countries? In table 4-2, we capture institutional differences by the following variables: the degree of centralization/coordination of collective bargaining, union density, and bargaining coverage (see chapter 5 for a detailed discussion of these indicators). Following OECD (1997), the sample of countries can be classified according to the level at which collective bargaining takes place (the firm, the industry, or the national level) and according to the degree of informal coordination between workers and employers. The countries are ranked from "1" (centralized/coordinated) through "2" (semicentralized/coordinated) to "3" (decentralized/uncoordinated) in column 1 of table 4-2. Excluding Japan and Ireland for the aforementioned reasons, countries with centralized/coordinated or decentralized/uncoordinated bargaining systems tend to have a higher markup than those with a semicentralized/coordinated bargaining system. The average markup in the last group is 1.6 percent versus 8.7 percent and 11.6 percent, respectively, in the other two groups.[6]

The markup can also vary depending on the percentage of wage- and salary-earners that are unionized (union density, column 2 in table 4-2 and the percentage of wage- and salary-earners covered by union agreements irrespective of whether or not they are members of unions (bargaining coverage, see column 3 in table 4-2). While union density per se appears to be largely unrelated to the wage markup (correlation coefficient of 0.02),[7] bargaining coverage is negatively correlated with the markup (correlation coefficient of −0.58). In other words, the more workers who are covered by a collective agreement, the smaller, other things being equal, the wage markup appears to be.[8] This result is largely driven by the fact that the United States has the largest wage markup and the lowest bargaining coverage (18 percent), and countries like the

---

6.   If a small markup is taken to indicate less distortionary conditions, this result runs prima facie counter to the proposition that a semicentralized bargaining system performs worse than both decentralized and centralized bargaining systems (Calmfors and Driffill 1988).

7.   Again, excluding Ireland and Japan.

8.   Of course, this result could also be caused by the fact that in countries where bargaining coverage is high, the union/nonunion membership markup underestimates the true impact of unionization.

Netherlands and Spain have a low markup and high bargaining coverage. Nevertheless, all this points to the possibility that the more workers become unionized or are covered by collective agreements, the lower is the markup that they can secure. This may be the case because the labor supply in the noncovered sector decreases when more workers become covered, pushing the nonunion wage up. Taking this argument one step further, we may say that unions are able to secure a high markup only where the marginal cost to society (in terms of impact on the macroeconomy) is small. In effect, unions are ultimately constrained by the wage share in the total economy: they can have wide coverage and a small markup or a high markup at the cost of coverage.

The estimates in tables 4-1 and 4-2 refer to a given point in time. An interesting additional question is whether the markup is stable over time or it fluctuates with economic conditions. This question has been investigated in only two countries—the United States and the United Kingdom. Blanchflower (1997) concludes that the wage markup in the United States has moved procyclically, but that it does not appear to have a trend over the period 1983–95.[9] Stewart (1995) finds that the markup in the United Kingdom has declined a bit during the 1980s.[10] These results suggest that union power has not been curtailed significantly, despite the reduction in union density observed over the same period in the two countries.[11]

Blanchflower and Freeman (1992) and Blanchflower (1996b) argue that the high and stable wage markup is one reason why union density has declined in the private sector in the United States.[12] The high wage markup, so the argument goes, has created substantial opposition from employers, which, together with a highly adversarial electoral process

---

9.   Historically, the wage markup has moved countercyclically in the United States. For example, it increased significantly during the Depression of the 1930s (Filer, Hamermesh, and Rees 1996: table 13.4). This can be related to the fact that union wage contracts are typically long-term contracts.

10.   The main reason for this decline is that unions have had a hard time establishing a wage markup in new firms (those started after 1984), whereas the markup in "old" firms (those that existed in 1984) is approximately the same in 1984 as in 1990. Moreover, the drop in the additional markup associated with pre-entry closed shops also contributed significantly to the overall drop in the average markup.

11.   Union density in the United States has declined from 27 percent in 1970 to 16 percent in 1994. The corresponding numbers for the United Kingdom are 45 percent in 1970 and 34 percent in 1994.

12.   This view has been challenged by, for example, Farber and Krueger (1992). They analyze the decline by focusing on the demand and supply of unionized jobs. The demand for unionized jobs arises from workers who would prefer a union job without being willing to invest in organizing a union to provide the job. The supply of union jobs arises from workers who are willing to invest in organizing unions, and it is affected by the legal framework and the general resistance of employers to unions. Contrary to the claim by

to determine union recognition,[13] makes it difficult to unionize new and expanding industries to make up for the contraction of old and union-ized sectors. Stewart (1991) investigates in detail whether the decline in unionization from 1980 to 1984 in the United Kingdom is related to the size of the wage markup. He finds little evidence of this. It is therefore likely that the decline in union density in the United Kingdom is caused by changes in labor market legislation and industrial structure during the period rather than by the size of the wage markup per se.

To gain more insight into this issue, we include in table 4-2 , column 4, information about the change in union density during the period 1970 to 1993 for the broader sample of countries. An "A" indicates a country where union density declined between 1970 and 1993; a "B" indicates increasing union density in the 1970s but declining thereafter; a "C" in-dicates declining density in the 1980s but stabilizing in the 1990s; and a "D" indicates increasing density throughout the whole period. The wage markup tends to be higher in those countries (groups A and B) that have had declining density rates in the 1980s and 1990s than in those coun-tries (groups C and D) that have had increasing or constant density rates in the 1990s. The average markup for the two groups is 11.8 percent and 4.5 percent, respectively.[14] Although these calculations are very crude and too static to indicate anything about causality, they do demonstrate that changes in union density may be related to the markup.

The Efficiency Cost of the Wage Markup

When unions are successful in getting a wage markup, workers tend to be displaced from the unionized sectors to nonunion sectors. As pointed out by Rees (1963), this creates a deadweight loss. A number of studies have estimated this deadweight loss and found it to be quite small. The original study by Rees (1963) estimates that the welfare loss in the United States in 1957 was only 0.14 percent of GDP. Johnson and Mieszkowski (1970) find a similar result. Freeman and Medoff (1984: chapter 3) calculate the cost of the average wage markup of 15 percent in the United States in 1980 to be between 0.2 and 0.4 percent of GDP. Studies that use large-scale Computable General Equilibrium (CGE)

Blanchflower and Freeman (1992) and others, Farber and Krueger find that demand forces are much more important than supply forces in explaining the decline and that changes in industry structure can account for only one-quarter of the decline.

13.   For example, there has been a significant increase in the number of states that enforce "right to work" laws, and at the national level, there have been changes in the interpretation of various labor laws, all of which have made it more difficult for new unions to organize.

14.   Excluding Ireland and Japan.

models find comparable small losses. DeFina (1983) uses a 12-sector CGE model to simulate the welfare loss associated with a 25 percent union/nonunion wage markup. He finds modest effects: the welfare loss is no larger than 0.2 percent of GDP. Interestingly, the U.S. results are similar to those for Australia, where the average markup is 7 to 17 percent and where 80 percent of the work force is covered by collective agreements. Christie (1992) estimates the welfare loss associated with the union/nonunion wage markup in Australia to be similar, at about 0.5 percent of GDP.

Variations in the Wage Markup

The average wage markup disguises the variations that exist across different types of workers or different types of collective bargaining. In this section, we review some of these issues. In particular, we consider how the wage markup varies across gender, ethnicity, occupation, skills, education, economic environment, and various characteristics of the collective bargaining system.

The Difference in the Markup for Women and Men

Unions are just one of many determinants of the gender wage gap. The gender wage gap is the percentage difference between the wage of a female worker and a male worker who otherwise have the same personal and workplace characteristics. The effect of unions arises in three ways: first, from different unionization rates among men and women; second, from the ability of unions to influence wages in some sectors but not in others; and third, from differences in the wage markup for men and women. The net effect of unions upon female wages relative to male wages is uncertain, and we shall not attempt to resolve the issue here. Instead, we review the evidence related to gender differences in the wage markup and a few studies that focus directly on the effect of unions on the gender wage gap. Although a higher wage markup for women than for men can reduce the gender wage gap, it can also decrease the wages of nonunionized women to such an extent that the gender wage gap actually increases.

In his survey of the U.S. literature, Lewis (1986) concludes that there is very little, if any, difference between the markup for female and male workers. Main and Reilly (1992) and Blanchflower and Freeman (1996) have recently confirmed this conclusion for the 1990s. The same result emerges from Australian studies (Christie 1992; Mulvey 1986). Most studies in Britain show that the impact of unions on women's wages is greater than that on men's wages (Blanchflower 1996b, 1997; Blanchflower and Freeman 1996; Main 1991; Main and Reilly 1992). A typical estimate is that the markup for women is 4 to 6 percentage points larger than that for men. However, a few studies (Green 1988; Yaron 1990) find the opposite result. In any case, taking into account the fact that women workers are less likely to be unionized than men workers, the net effect on the average gender wage gap is likely to be small (Doiron and Riddell 1994). Evidence from other OECD and middle-income countries unambiguously supports the view that the wage markup is greater for women. Nakumura, Sato, and Kamiya (1988), in their study of Japan, find a wage markup of 10 percent for women but fails to find any for men. Likewise, Schmidt (1995) shows that the small average wage markup in West Germany is mainly due to a wage markup among unionized female workers. The findings for Mexico by Panagides and Patrinos (1994) suggest that the markup for women is 9.8 percentage points higher than that for men with similar characteristics. Finally, Moll (1993) finds that the wage markup among black blue-collar workers in South Africa in 1985 is about 11 percentage points higher for women than for men (31 percent compared to 19 percent).

Some studies focus directly on the gender gap rather than on gender differences in the markup. Simpson (1985), for example, estimates the gender wage gaps in the unionized and nonunionized sectors in Canada. He finds that the gap is 22.9 percent in the unionized sector and 20.3 percent in the nonunionized sector. This indicates that unions have little impact on the gender wage gap. Doiron and Riddell (1994) incorporate the effect from the increase in the female unionization rate and the decrease in the male unionization rate in their analysis of the gender wage gap in Canada. They show that, had it not been for union effects, the gender wage gap would have increased by 7 percent in the 1980s. Also, the gender wage gap in the nonunion sector makes a larger contribution to the gender wage gap than does the gap in the union sector. Overall, this suggests that unions in Canada have helped to reduce gender discrimination, albeit this may not be directly related to differences in the wage markup for the two groups of workers. Standing (1992) compares the wage ratio of male and female workers in nonunionized and unionized firms in Malaysia. His result suggests that the presence of a union reduces the ratio of male to female wages, and he concludes "the data gives *prima facie* support to the view that in terms of wages, at least, women gain more than proportionately from unionization" (Standing 1992: 341).

Differences in the Markup by Ethnic Group

Discrimination among workers with different ethnic backgrounds but otherwise similar productivity characteristics can lead to a wage differential. Here we are interested in the impact of unions on the markup for workers with different ethnic characteristics.

In the United States, it is not clear whether there is a substantial difference between the wage markup for white and nonwhite workers. Some studies fail to find any difference, whereas others find that the markup is 5 to 10 percentage points higher for blacks than for whites (Lewis 1986: chapter 7). In the United Kingdom, the sparse evidence available shows that a nonwhite unionized worker gets a higher markup than a similar white worker (Blanchflower 1997). In South Africa, Dabalen (1998) finds that white workers get a markup of about 30 percent, whereas the markup for black workers is in the range of 16 to 20 percent. Butcher and Rouse (2001) find that after controlling for worker heterogeneity the markup for both groups is somewhat smaller, in particular for white workers (10 percent). As we discuss below, these numbers hide interesting differences between workers with different skills.

Patrinos and Sakellariou (1992) decompose the difference between the average wage of employed Indians and non-Indians in Canada into (a) the part that is explained by differences in income-generating characteristics such as years of schooling, experience, unionization, and other variables and (b) the part that cannot be explained by these variables.[15] The unexplained part is taken as an indicator of discrimination against Indians in the labor market. They find, on the one hand, that unions marginally reduce discrimination (but other variables such as education and experience are much more important). On the other hand, since Indians are less likely to be unionized than non-Indians, this tends to increase the total earnings differential between the two groups. Panagides and Patrinos (1994) investigate the impact of unions on the wages of indigenous people in Mexico. They include a variable in their wage regressions for unionized and nonunionized workers that measures the percentage of the population in a particular county who are indigenous. They show that a worker who lives in a county with a large indigenous population gets a bigger wage markup than a similar worker living in a less "indigenous" county.

The Private versus the Public Sector

It is unclear if public sector workers are in a weaker position than private sector workers to exert wage pressure. Historically, they have been restricted from forming unions in many industrial countries. Even when public sector unions are legal, they are often legally barred from striking. This suggests that the average wage markup in the public sector may be smaller than the corresponding markup in the private sector. On the other hand, public goods and publicly provided private goods are produced in an environment with no or little competition. Moreover, producers in the

---

15. Indians refer to Canada's Aboriginal or Native people.

public sector are not motivated by a profit concern; rather, they have a politically imposed budget constraint. The lack of competitive pressure and soft budget constraints makes it easier to pass on the costs of high wages and overstaffing to taxpayers. Finally, as argued by Freeman (1986), public sector unions may be able to influence employers' behavior through the political process. In many developing countries, unionization is concentrated in the public sector, and there are few legal constraints on the kind of behavior that these unions may engage in. In such an environment, unions are able to exercise substantial political pressure. This may contribute significantly to the rent-seeking cost of unions in addition to the impact it may have on the wage markup.

In this section, we examine studies that compare the wage markup between the public and private sectors in Canada, the United Kingdom, and the United States. Most studies divide individual workers into two groups. One group contains all employees (police officers, firefighters, truck drivers, teachers, white-collar public administration workers, and so on) or a subset of employees (such as craftspeople or white-collar workers) in the public sector. The other group contains all workers in the economy. Each of these groups is then divided into unionized and nonunionized workers, and the wage markups for workers in the public and private sectors are estimated. Lewis (1990) identifies a number of specific problems associated with estimating the public sector wage markup. First, in the private sector, wage and working conditions of unionized workers are determined by a union-negotiated contract, whereas non-union workers are typically excluded from the benefits of the union contract. In the public sector, the "wage-comparability" criterion is often used, and it is not uncommon for both union and nonunion workers to get the same wage and working conditions. This makes it more difficult to classify workers according to how their wage is being determined and makes it preferable to use the recognition markup rather than a membership markup. Second, the work force mix differs between the private and public sectors. For example, the work force in the public sector generally consists of a disproportionately large share of white-collar workers. Since the markup for white-collar workers tends to be smaller than that for blue-collar workers, failing to take the work force mix into account can underestimate the markup in the public sector. Third, workers in the two sectors receive different amounts of fringe benefits.

Lewis (1990) reviews 75 U.S. studies that have estimated the wage markup for the public sector at large or for some specific groups of workers within the public sector (such as teachers). After correcting for the problems discussed above, he concludes "[t]he mean wage gap [wage markup] (after adjustments for fringe benefits and workforce mix) in the public sector in 1973–84 moved approximately parallel to that in all sectors but at a level lower by about 0.03 to 0.07. I estimate that the public-sector gap in this period averaged about 0.08–0.12..." (Lewis 1990: 321). More recently, Blanchflower (1997), who uses data from 1993–94, obtained a similar result. Moreover, Lewis (1990) finds that, within the public sector, the wage markup is lowest for federal employees and highest for employees of local governments in the United States. In fact, the average markup for workers employed by local governments in 1973–84 was slightly higher than the economy-wide average. Green (1988) considers the difference in the wage markup for workers in the public and private sectors in the United Kingdom. He finds that the wage markup is smaller for both manual and nonmanual workers in the public sector than in the private sector. Blanchflower (1996b, 1997) and Blanchflower and Freeman (1992), however, find that the wage markup in the private and public sectors is very similar (the difference being about 2 percentage points in favor of the private sector) in the United Kingdom. Robinson and Tomes (1984) and Simpson (1985) find a similar result for Canada.

The Markup for Workers with Different Skills

Collective bargaining can insert a wedge between worker productivity and wages. Although this can be desirable as a way to avoid wage inequality from a societal point of view, it can also distort the relative wages of skilled and unskilled workers or the relative rewards for different types of jobs. As a consequence, resources can be misallocated, and the resulting efficiency loss has to be traded off against the distributive gain.

In the United States (Lewis 1986: chapter 7) and the United Kingdom (Booth 1995: table 6.1), manual workers get a larger markup than nonmanual workers. Likewise, semiskilled workers get a larger markup than skilled workers. Similar results have been obtained in Canada (Simpson 1985). In South Africa, the wage markup for workers with different skills varies between different ethnic groups. For example, the average wage markup for unskilled *nonwhite* workers is 19 percent, while the wage markup for semiskilled nonwhite workers is much smaller and the markup for skilled nonwhite workers is practically zero. On the other hand, semiskilled and skilled *white* workers got a wage markup of 13 percent in 1985 (Moll 1993). Moll (1993: 256) concludes that "black unions tended to compress wages by skill level."[16] Although Dabalen

---

16.   The comparison between black and white workers with respect to the markup for different skill groups should not be carried too far. This is because the sample of white workers is small and also because white and black workers are probably distributed differently across industries.

(1998) finds somewhat smaller estimates, his study confirms the general pattern observed by Moll (1993). In Malaysia, unions reduce the intrafirm wage differential between skilled and unskilled workers. In particular, industry unions tend to reduce the differential between workers with different skills more than company unions do (Standing 1992).

Unions, Wage Dispersion, and the Return to Schooling

The facts that unionized workers get a wage markup and that unionization is concentrated among low-paid workers suggest that unions reduce the wage dispersion *across* an economy. Moreover, the impact of unions on the wage dispersion *within* the unionized sector can also contribute to low overall wage dispersion. For example, the differences between the wage markup for different skill groups (see above) indicate that unions contribute to the compression of wages within the unionized sectors of the economy. There are many reasons why unions may be keen to promote a compressed wage scale across different groups of workers employed within the unionized sectors of the economy. One reason may be that they have egalitarian wage goals. Egalitarian wage goals can arise if productivity differs among union members and if the median member has low (compared to average) productivity. Under these circumstances, a democratic union tends to enter wage contracts that compress the wage structure (Freeman 1980b).

Evidence from the United Kingdom and the United States indicates that unions reduce wage dispersion significantly between industries, between (similar) firms within an industry, and among workers within a firm (Freeman 1980b; Gosling and Machin 1994).[17] Evidence from Mexico points in the same direction. Panagides and Patrinos (1994) compare the Gini coefficient associated with the wage distribution for unionized and nonunionized workers.[18] For nonunionized workers, the estimated Gini coefficient is 42.1. The corresponding number for unionized workers is 33.5.

The fact that unions tend to reduce the wage dispersion can affect the decisions people make about their children's and their own education. These decisions depend on a number of factors. One important factor is the return to education in terms of higher (future) wages. If unions reduce the return to schooling, say, by compressing the wage differential between workers with different skills, they can have an adverse impact

---

17.   In the United Kingdom, the bulk of the overall rise in earnings inequality is, however, due to a large increase in earnings dispersion across nonunion establishments.

18.   The Gini coefficient is a measure of the degree of wage inequality. The larger the value of the coefficient, the more unequal is the distribution of wages.

on the formation of human capital. On the other hand, when the relative wage of unskilled workers increases, firms substitute away from unskilled workers. To avoid being unemployed, (unskilled) workers have to acquire more skills, so the compression of the wage distribution may induce more, rather than less, human capital formation.[19] The empirical evidence suggests that the wage markup is usually higher for less educated workers in countries such as Canada, the United Kingdom, and the United States.[20] The same pattern appears in Mexico, where Panagides and Patrinos (1994: 18) show that the wage markup decreases as the education level of workers increases.

The Economic Environment

The economic realities facing firms can make it difficult for unions to get a high wage markup. As discussed in chapter 3, competitive pressure from both the product market and the nonunion labor market can be particularly effective in serving this role.

A number of studies from the United States and the United Kingdom have investigated the effect of competitive pressure on the wage markup. Most of these studies use industry concentration as a proxy for a firm's market power. Concentration as a measure of competitiveness has been proxied by either the volume of sales or employment accounted for by the three or five largest firms in the industry or some more sophisticated measure such as an index of concentration. In the United States, the majority of studies (Lewis 1986: 154) find a negative correlation between industry concentration and the wage markup in manufacturing industries. This is also the case in the United Kingdom (Stewart 1983). In a study of Canada, Martinello and Meng (1992) find indirect evidence that industry characteristics such as concentration, import penetration, and labor substitutability have little impact on the wage markup.

These results do not support the theoretical predictions. However, the relationship between monopoly power and the wage markup can be masked in these estimates if wages are high in concentrated industries even in the absence of unions. For example, this would be the case if firms in these industries wish to forestall unionization. Another reason is that firms in concentrated sectors would like to escape possible enforcement of competitive laws or they want to avoid the bad press associated with high profits and low wages. As argued by Sapsford and

---

19.   See Ravn and Sørensen (1997) for a recent model that makes this type of argument in a model with a minimum wage that compresses the wage distribution from below.

20.   See Blanchflower (1997), Booth (1995), Christie (1992), Lewis (1986), Panagides and Patrinos (1994), and Simpson (1985).

Tzannatos (1993: 203–4), these reasons may be more apparent than real. For example, the fear of provoking the response of the competitive authorities is hypothetical in many countries where there is little faith in competition laws and little effort is spent on enforcing them. Also, firms may receive better press coverage by spending part of their excess profits on health and safety improvements in the workplace or by donating to charities rather than by paying higher wages. Another interpretation of the evidence is that firms in concentrated industries use their monopoly rent to withstand the wage demands of unions. This may induce workers to be content with greater job security and other nonmonetary benefits as a substitute for high wages. Finally, the industry concentration ratio may not be a good proxy for a firm's monopoly power in the product market.

This suspicion seems to be confirmed by a few studies that have used indicators other than industry concentration to measure the monopoly power of firms. These studies find that the wage markup is larger in firms with monopoly power than in those without it. First, Mishel (1986) uses a mixture of industry concentration ratios and a subjective measure of entry barriers to the industry as a proxy for monopoly power in a sample of unionized U.S. manufacturing firms (in 1968 to 1972). He finds that the wage markup is significantly higher in noncompetitive industries than in competitive ones. Second, Stewart (1990) measures the degree of product market competition among U.K. firms by simply asking the management of each firm about the number of competitors that they are facing in the product market. This provides a firm-specific measure of monopoly power. When it is defined in this way, he finds that competition in the product market significantly reduces the average wage markup. In particular, in firms that operate in a competitive product market, the wage markup is, on average, zero. On the other hand, firms that have little or no competition in the product market grant a wage markup in the range of 8 to 10 percent. Moreover, unions are unable to create a wage markup in firms that primarily operate, in international markets. In addition, unions are able to create a markup only in industries that are sheltered from foreign competition when the whole industry is unionized.

The Design of Collective Bargaining

We have seen that workers, on average, get a wage markup if they are members of a union or otherwise have their pay conditions determined by collective agreements. However, the size of the markup may depend on how collective bargaining is organized. In this section, we focus on the impact that different bargaining structures and institutions have on the wage markup in addition to the membership or coverage effect. We consider four aspects of the institutional framework:

- The extent of unionism (average union density in the industry or the percentage of firms in the industry that recognizes a union).
- The level at which bargaining takes place (the firm, industry, or the national level).
- Multiunionism (more than one union can potentially represent the same worker).
- Closed shops (a worker can obtain or retain a particular job only if he or she is a member of a particular union).

The extent of unionism. There seems to be a strong relationship between the extent of unionism in an industry (or occupation) and the wage markup. In industries where unionization is low in terms of either density or the percentage of firms that recognize a union, unions generally have little impact on wages. This is because attempts to raise the wages paid by a few unionized employers (above what their competitors pay) put union employers at a severe disadvantage in the product market. This increases employers' resistance to union wage pressure and encourages the union to moderate its wage demands. On the other hand, in industries where almost all firms are unionized, unions will have more bargaining power and will therefore be able to secure a higher wage markup. This is known as the "extent of unionism" effect (Green 1988: 186).

Many studies have estimated this effect in the United States. They use union density in specific industries as the relevant indicator (the percentage of all workers in the industry who are members of a union). The main finding is that union density increases the membership markup, although there is substantial disagreement about the magnitude of this effect (Lewis 1986: chapter 7). In Canada in the late 1970s, the wages of otherwise identical unionized Canadian workers in industries with high union density were 13 percent higher than in industries with almost no unionized workers (Robinson and Tomes 1984). Green (1988) investigates the relationship between the membership wage markup and the union density of the relevant industry in the United Kingdom at the beginning of the 1980s. He finds that the wage markup is always larger in industries with more than 70 percent union density. For example, in these industries, the (hourly) wage markup for manual workers is 34 percent, compared to 7 percent in industries where union density is less than 30 percent. The corresponding markups for nonmanual workers are 13 percent and practically zero. These findings are consistent with earlier results (Stewart 1983).

In the United States, there is no significant difference between union density and coverage of collective agreements. In the United Kingdom, on the other hand, a large number of workers have their pay conditions determined by collective agreements without actually being members of a union. Therefore, focusing on the membership wage markup may bias not only the estimate of the wage markup itself but also the estimate of the extent of the unionism effect. More recent British studies take this into account and analyze the relationship between the recognition wage markup and union density at the establishment level. Metcalf and Stewart (1992) find that the recognition wage markup (for semiskilled manual workers in 1984) is significant only for firms where more than 95 percent of the work force is unionized. The markup is in the range of 7 to 10 percent. In firms where a smaller fraction of semiskilled workers are union members, the wage markup is insignificant. This suggests that workers in a workplace where management does recognize a union benefit in terms of higher wages only if almost all the workers in the workplace are actually organized in unions.

The level at which collective bargaining takes place. The level at which collective bargaining takes place affects how workers and employers interact, and this has implications for the size of the wage markup. From the discussion in chapter 3 of centralization of collective bargaining, we would expect the wage markup to be higher when collective bargaining is at the industry level rather than at the firm level. Using individual worker data from U.K. establishments in 1980 and 1984, Stewart (1987) fails to find any evidence that the level of bargaining affects the markup for semiskilled and skilled manual workers. This is in contrast to earlier studies (Mulvey 1976). Mishel (1986) found, for example, that the wage markup was higher in U.S. industries that used centralized bargaining in 1968–72 than in industries that used firm-level bargaining.

Standing (1992) analyzes the impact of industrial and company unions on the wage markup in Malaysian manufacturing firms in 1988. In Standing's terminology, an industrial union is a union that organizes workers from a given industry irrespective of their trade. A company union, on the other hand, is a union that only organizes workers who are employed in the relevant firm—again irrespective of their trade. He finds that the average wage markup paid by a firm that deals with an industrial union is 19.7 percent, compared to 14.9 percent in firms that deal with a company union. Bhattacherjee (1987) examines similar issues for India. He uses a data set of 119 plant-level agreements between manufacturing firms and blue-collar unions in Greater Bombay and Pune in 1978–84. He distinguishes two types of unions: (a) external unions (unions that are explicitly affiliated with a trade union federation, which in turn is affiliated with a political party) and (b) independent plant-based unions (unions run and managed by workers employed in the plant). His main finding is that members of independent plant-based unions get significantly higher wages and bonuses than other workers. While these findings may reflect the specific circumstances that prevailed in Bombay at the time of the study, they do suggest that plant unions (the Japanese model of industrial relations) do not always produce wage constraint.

Multiunionism. The prime source of information on the effect of multiunionism is the United Kingdom where multiunionism has traditionally played an important role. In the 1980s, about 30 percent of all unionized plants in the private sector recognized more than one union for collective bargaining purposes. Under multiunionism, the unions may bargain together (multiple bargaining) or separately (separate bargaining) with management. Stewart (1987) finds that multiunionism is associated with a higher wage markup in the United Kingdom. Subsequent studies have refined this result. Machin, Stewart, and van Reenen (1993) have shown that it is not multiunionism per se that is associated with the additional wage markup; it is the combination of multiunionism and separate collective bargaining that produces the additional wage markup. If all the unions that represent workers at a given workplace bargain together, then the wage markup is no larger than in firms where workers (of the same type) are represented by a single union.

Closed shops. A closed shop exists when an employee can obtain or retain a particular job only if he or she is a member of a particular union. The closed shop can be either pre- or post-entry. A pre-entry closed shop requires that the employee is accepted as a member of the relevant union ("holds a union card") *before* he or she can be employed in the particular trade. Historically, craft unions have managed to run a pre-entry closed shop.[21] One example is the International Typographical Union in the United States, which at its peak required that all individuals hired for the composing room must already have union cards. A post-entry closed shop requires that the employee joins the union upon getting a specific job. In the United Kingdom, post-entry closed shops have been important in industries such as metal engineering, transport, and communications (Stevens, Millward, and Smart 1989). From a theoretical point of view, a closed shop increases a union's control over labor supply and as a result its bargaining power.[22] The question, therefore, is whether the presence of a closed shop increases the wage markup over and above the basic recognition or membership effect.

---

21.   Some professions such as doctors and journalists regulate themselves and are effectively running pre-entry closed shops.

22.   A British study by Stevens, Millward, and Smart (1989) finds that employees in pre-entry closed shops face a formidable range of sanctions if they lose or give up their union membership. For example, about two-fifths of workers expected to be dismissed or made to resign by their employers, and a quarter argued that the union did limit entry by restricting the number or types of people that it takes into membership.

In the United Kingdom, closed shops used to be common before various changes in the industrial relations framework took place during the 1980s.[23] In 1989, about 12 percent of all employees worked under some kind of closed shop arrangement. Half of these were pre-entry and half were post-entry closed shops (Stevens, Millward, and Smart 1989). Stewart (1987, 1991) uses data from the 1980 and 1984 workplace survey to analyze the effect of closed shops on the wage markup. Stewart (1991) finds that the pre-entry premium on semiskilled pay is about 14 percent and the post-entry premium is about 3 percent relative to the pay in an establishment with union recognition but no form of closed shop. Metcalf and Stewart (1992) investigate if the wage premium found in earlier studies was due to the presence of a closed shop per se or if it arose because union membership by definition is high in establishments that run a closed shop. To this end, they use a British workplace survey from 1984. Their main finding is that the post-entry closed shop does not increase the wage markup above what it would have been had the majority of the firm's workers been unionized. On the other hand, pre-entry closed shops can increase the wage markup by as much as 100 percent. They conclude, "[T]he pre-entry variety is—on the pay dimension—a separate institutional form with an effect additional to density. This is, however, not so for the post-entry closed shop, which brings no extra reward in terms of pay in addition to that resulting from high density" (Metcalf and Stewart 1992: 507). However, subsequent research using a British workplace survey from 1990 (Stewart 1995) finds that the premium associated with the pre-entry closed shop has been reduced and is roughly the same as that found in firms where management recommends union membership.

Other Union Effects

In this section, we examine the impact of unions on other aspects of economic performance than wages. These include employment growth, hours worked, productivity (level and growth), job mobility, implementation of new technology, spending on R&D, training, profitability, fringe benefits, mode of pay, and provision of pensions.

Table 4-3 summarizes our conclusions and provides a classification of union effects on nonwage dimensions of economic performance according to the degree of confidence that we have in them. In column one, we list the relevant dimension of economic performance. In column two, we

---

23.   In the late 1980s, the British government banned pre-entry and post-entry closed shops.

Table 4-3. Summary of Union Effects on Nonwage Dimensions of Economic Performance

Indicator	Union effect	Number of studies	Variation in results	Evidence from	Degree of robustness
Hours worked	Unions reduce total and normal hours but increase paid overtime.	25	Agreement	Australia, Canada, Germany, Ireland, Italy, Japan, Netherlands, New Zealand, Spain, Switzerland, United Kingdom, and United States	High
Job mobility	Unions reduce voluntary turnover and increase job tenure and temporary layoffs.	16	Agreement	Australia, Japan, Malaysia, United Kingdom, and United States	High
Profitability	Unions reduce profitability. The effect is larger when firms have product-market power.	18	Agreement	Japan, United Kingdom, and United States	High
Productivity level	Unions have a negative impact on productivity levels unless (a) unionized firms operate in competitive product markets and/or (b) industrial relations in the workplace are of high quality.	28	Disagreement	Germany, Japan, Malaysia, United Kingdom, and United States	Low
Productivity growth	Unions have an ambiguous effect. In the United States, the effect is nonpositive. In the United Kingdom, the impact depends on the time period.	18	Disagreement	United Kingdom and United States	Low
New technology	There is little or no difference between unionized and nonunionized firms with respect to the implementation of new technology.	6	Some disagreement	Canada, Malaysia, United Kingdom, and United States	Low
Training	Unions tend to increase company-related training.	4	Some disagreement	Malaysia, United Kingdom, and United States	Low

(table continues on following page)

Table 4-3 continued

Indicator	Union effect	Number of studies	Variation in results	Evidence from	Degree of robustness
Pay systems	Unions reduce the use of individual performance pay and increase the use of seniority pay.	3	Agreement	Malaysia, United Kingdom, and United States	Low
Employment growth	Unions reduce employment growth.	8	Some disagreement	Canada, Jamaica, Malaysia, United Kingdom, and United States	Medium
Physical investments	Unions reduce the investment rate of physical capital.	6	Agreement	United Kingdom and United States	Medium
Spending on R&D	Unions reduce spending on R&D.	6	Agreement	United Kingdom and United States	Medium
Employment-related benefits	Unions increase employment-related benefits such as severance pay, paid holidays, paid sick leave, and pension plans.	8	Agreement	Australia, Japan, Malaysia, United Kingdom, and United States	Medium

Source: See text. The judgement of robustness is that of the authors.

summarize our evaluation of the effect of unions on the relevant dimension of economic performance. In columns three to six, we provide information about the robustness of the results. First, we indicate how many studies we identified and surveyed (column three).[24] Second, we indicate if there is agreement among the studies about the direction of the union effect (column four). Third, we list the set of countries from which evidence is available (column five). In the last column, we provide our evaluation of the robustness of the results. The degree of robustness can be high, medium, or low. It is said to be *high* if (a) there is agreement about the direction of the union effect, (b) if more than 10 studies can be identified, and (c) if the evidence from the United States and the United Kingdom is confirmed by evidence from other countries. The degree of robustness is said to be *low* if there is disagreement about the direction of the union effect or fewer than five studies have been identified and surveyed. The degree of robustness is said to be *medium* if (a) there is agreement among the studies about the sign of the union effect, and (b) between 5 and 10 studies, including a study from at least one country other than the United States and the United Kingdom, can be identified.

Unions and Employment

The wage markup reduces total employment as long as the demand curve of labor in the unionized sector of the economy is sloping downward and the management of unionized firms retains the right to manage (that is, management independently decides on employment after wages have been agreed with the union). However, as pointed out in the section in chapter 3, the adverse employment effect can be reduced and even reversed if (a) unions and firms bargain over wages *and* employment and enter an efficient contract or if (b) firms have monopsony power in the absence of collective bargaining. Oswald and Turnbull (1985) and Oswald (1993) have investigated if unions and firms typically bargain over employment. They find that this is rarely the case in either the United Kingdom or the United States. In the United States, many contracts explicitly state that the right to determine employment remains with the management. While this is not true in the United Kingdom, U.K. unions do not generally bargain over employment.[25] However, although the employment level per se is not subject to formal

---

24.   With respect to the evidence from the United States and the United Kingdom, we have drawn heavily on the surveys provided by Bellman (1992), Booth (1995), Lewis (1986), and Pencavel (1991).

25.   There are exceptions such as in the printing and mining sectors.

bargaining, recruitment, staffing norms, redundancy pay, and deployment are included in formal bargaining, and this can have indirect effects on employment (Booth 1995: table 4.1). It is possible to test econometrically the *right to manage model* (unions push up wages and reduce employment) against the *efficient bargaining model* (unions push up wages and employment).[26] The results consistently reject both models. Ulph and Ulph (1990: 102) conclude "on the whole neither theory seems to be able to account satisfactorily for the data on negotiated wages and their associated employment levels." Although it is tempting to argue that the truth should lie somewhere in the middle, data limitations and the procedure used to test the two models may be seriously flawed (Booth 1995: 137–40).[27]

Another way to assess the impact of unions on employment is to look at employment growth. Here the available evidence from Canada, Jamaica, Malaysia, the United Kingdom, and the United States suggests that employment grows more slowly in unionized firms than in nonunionized ones. Studies from Canada, the United Kingdom, and the United States[28] typically find a growth differential in the range of 3 to 5 percentage points per year in favor of nonunionized firms.[29] Evidence

---

26.   See Alogoskoufis and Manning (1991), Bean and Turnbull (1988), Brown and Ashenfelter (1986), Card (1986), MacCurdy and Pencavel (1986), and others.

27.   In short, the idea of the test is this. If the right to manage model is true, then conditional on the wage negotiated in the contract, the alternative wage should have no independent impact on employment. On the other hand, if the efficient contract model is true, then the alternative wage should have an impact on employment. Unfortunately, the different impact of the alternative wage on employment depends on the specification of the union's objective function (Pencavel 1991: 210). Moreover, as pointed out by Oswald (1993), the difference between the efficient contract model and the right to manage model disappears when membership dynamics are taken into account.

28.   Boal and Pencavel (1994), Bronars, Deere, and Tracy (1994), Dunne and MacPherson (1994), Freeman and Kleiner (1990), Lalonde, Marschke, and Troski (1996), and Leonard (1992) provide evidence from the United States. Long (1993) estimates the differential for a sample of Canadian firms. Blanchflower et al (1991) provide evidence from the United Kingdom. The study by Blanchflower et al (1991) has been subject to criticism. Machin and Wadhwani (1991) argue that the difference in the growth rate of employment in unionized and nonunionized firms is due to the fact that unionized firms experienced a reduction in restrictive practices during the sample period 1980–84. This implies that unionized firms were more likely than nonunionized firms to lay off workers during this period. This strongly suggests that the estimated effect is associated with an adjustment to a long-run equilibrium rather than with an equilibrium position per se.

29.   In their study of coal-mining data from West Virginia during the period 1897–1938, Boal and Pencavel (1994), however, find that the employment growth differential is approximately zero if the variation in working days is explicitly taken into account. Machin and Wadhwani (1991) find, using U.K. data, that employment grew faster in unionized establishments in the 1970s. Blanchflower and Burgess (1996) find that unions have a negative effect on employment in the United Kingdom but not in Australia.

on the employment growth differential is mixed in Malaysia. The employment growth differential is about 5 percentage points per year in firms that bargain with industrial unions but is insignificant in firms that deal with a company union (Standing 1992). Rama (1998) estimates the employment differential between sectors with high and low union membership rates for Jamaica over the period 1986–93 to be 2 to 5 percentage points per year. He argues that the most plausible explanation for the growth differential is slow productivity growth in the unionized sectors of the Jamaican economy.

This growth differential is quite substantial and may well represent disequilibrium phenomena. Rama (1998) provides a number of potential explanations for the observed employment growth differential:

- It takes time and effort to organize a union. Consequently, at a given point in time, old firms are more likely to be covered by unions than newer firms are. If newer firms expand faster than old firms, we would expect to observe higher employment growth in the newer, nonunionized firms.
- Unions are more likely to be concentrated in sectors that enjoy large rents. If these sectors are less dynamic because of monopoly inefficiencies and their activities are limited by the size of the domestic market, employment would tend to grow more slowly in these sectors.
- Unions may encourage labor hoarding by increasing hiring and firing costs. This would make unionized firms more reluctant to hire new workers during a boom, thus reducing employment growth over the cycle.
- Labor costs grow faster in unionized firms than in nonunionized ones.
- Productivity grows slower in unionized firms than in nonunionized ones.

Voluntary Turnover, Layoffs, and Job Tenure

The evidence from Australia, Japan, Malaysia, the United Kingdom, and the United States unanimously shows that voluntary turnover (measured by the "quit" rate) is lower and job tenure is longer in unionized firms than in nonunionized ones.[30] Freeman and Medoff (1984: 109–10) estimate the welfare gain associated with a reduction in labor turnover to be equivalent to a 0.2 to 0.3 percent increase in GDP in the United

---

30. See Elias and Blanchflower (1989), Freeman (1980a), Kupferschmidt and Swidensky (1989), Miller and Mulvey (1991, 1993), Muramatsu (1984), Osawa (1989), and Standing (1992).

States in the 1980s. For unionized firms, they estimate the gain to be equivalent to a 1 to 2 percent reduction in costs. To calculate the gain to workers, Freeman and Medoff (1984) first calculate the increase in wages necessary to reduce the nonunion quit rate to the union quit rate, and, second, they weight this by the difference between the quit rate in the unionized and nonunionized sectors. While these calculations are crude, it is interesting to notice that the welfare gain associated with participatory benefits of this kind is of the same order of magnitude as the estimated monopoly cost of unions. As pointed out by Freeman and Medoff (1984), it should be kept in mind, however, that the participatory benefit accrues to organized workers (and firms) only, whereas the monopoly cost of unions is borne by society at large.

While voluntary turnover tends to be lower in unionized firms than elsewhere, unions increase the use of layoffs, particularly temporary layoffs. In a study of layoff patterns in U.S. manufacturing firms in the 1960s and 1970s, Freeman and Medoff (1984: chapter 7) find that unions significantly alter the firm's choice between layoffs, wages, and hours worked in response to business cycle fluctuations. Unionized firms adjust by making temporary layoffs rather than by reducing weekly hours (work sharing) or wages.[31] In particular, unionized (blue-collar) workers are 50 to 60 percent more likely to be laid off temporarily than nonunionized workers. One explanation for this may be the fact that junior workers can be laid off more easily. Also, senior workers typically have more influence on the union's policy than junior workers. Faced with the choice between a reduction in their earnings or a temporary layoff of junior workers, unions are likely to prefer layoffs. Another explanation is that the cost of temporary layoffs can be shifted onto the unemployment benefit system. As long as there is less than a 100 percent experience rating (in other words, as long as the amount that firms contribute to unemployment benefits is less than the costs of the unemployment that they generate), those firms with above-average layoffs are subsidized at the expense of firms with below-average layoffs. Allen (1988) points to an interesting difference between the private and public sectors. While it is true that the existence of unions increases layoffs in the private sector, the opposite is true in the public sector. Public sector unions do not increase the wages of their members as much as private sector unions do. Instead, they reduce layoffs and protect employment.

---

31.   Temporary layoffs refer to a situation in which a worker is laid off for a shorter period of time (less than a month) and is recalled or rehired by the same firm.

Unions and Hours Worked

The effect of unions on the total number of hours worked by their members (compared to nonunionized workers) is not a priori clear. On the one hand, unions typically demand lower normal hours, more holidays, and so on. Conversely, they may be able to secure overtime work at higher rates of pay.

The union/nonunion hours differential has been extensively studied in the United States and the United Kingdom.[32] Overall, the finding is that unions reduce the total number of hours worked. In particular, the evidence suggests that workers in unionized firms work fewer normal hours. Moreover, unions reduce the number of unpaid overtime hours and, in some cases, increase the amount of paid overtime work (Oswald and Walker 1993; Trejo 1993). Furthermore, Green (1995) provides evidence that unions increase the likelihood that workers receive paid holidays and finds that unionized workers get, on average, almost an additional week of holidays compared to nonunionized workers in the United Kingdom. Finally, Blanchflower (1996b) estimates the union/nonunion total hours differential for 14 OECD countries in 1985–93.[33] He confirms the general result that unionized workers work less than nonunionized ones in all but two countries (Spain and Switzerland). The estimates range from a one- to two-hour differential per week in the United States and the United Kingdom to a four- to six-hour differential per week in Austria and Ireland.

Unions and Profitability

It is a commonly held view that unions reduce the profitability of firms because they appropriate part of the rent that would otherwise have been available to shareholders. The fact that unions are able to get a wage markup supports this view. As pointed out by Clark (1984), however, it is unwise to deduce the effect of unions on profitability by looking at the wage markup alone. This is because the union's ability to extract rent from a firm depends on the bargaining power of the union *and* on the size of the rent. The bargaining power and the size of the rent in turn

---

32.   See Lewis (1986: table 6.5) for a summary of 16 studies for the United States. See also DiNardo (1991), Earle and Pencavel (1990), Oswald and Walker (1993), Perloff and Sickles (1987), and Trejo (1993).

33.   They are Australia, Austria, Canada, Germany, Ireland, Italy, Japan, Netherlands, New Zealand, Norway, Spain, Switzerland, the United Kingdom, and the United States.

depend on a mixture of factors, including the structure of collective bargaining, the structure of the product market, the production technology used, and so on. In addition, by improving morale and job satisfaction among workers and by facilitating worker-employer cooperation, unions can contribute positively to profitability, as discussed in chapter 3. Therefore, instead of trying to capture a given rent, unions may help to create profits from which they can achieve wage gains (Filer, Hamermesh, and Rees 1996: 506).

A large number of studies have estimated the impact of unions on profitability. These studies use a number of different measures of profitability such as price/cost margins, net (of wages) return to capital, Tobin's q,[34] and subjective profitability judgments by management and estimate the impact using industry, firm, or stock market data. Bellman (1992) surveys 14 studies from the United States. All find that unions have a negative impact on profitability as measured by one or more of the indicators mentioned above. The impact tends to be larger in industries or firms that have some monopoly power in the product market. Some of the evidence suggests that the unions' share of monopoly profits may be as large as between 47 and 77 percent (Karier 1988). While these figures are hardly representative, they do show that under specific circumstances unions are able to appropriate a substantial share of monopoly profits. Booth (1995: table 7.6) surveys seven studies from the United Kingdom. While a few of them find that unions haves no impact on profitability, the general impression is that unions have a significant negative impact on profitability in British manufacturing firms. This adverse impact is larger when firms have some product market power. A Japanese study (Brunello 1992) finds that unions reduce the rate of return on equity by 20 to 25 percent. The ratio of profits to sales is reduced by about 40 percent.

The effect of unions on profitability seems to be clear: unions reduce profitability. The evidence reviewed above shows that the most pronounced union effects are found in industries where firms have monopoly power. This suggests that unions typically share in supernormal profits rather than cutting into normal profits (Reynolds 1986).

Productivity Differentials

As discussed in chapter 3, unions can contribute positively to labor productivity by improving work morale, facilitating cooperation with man-

---

34.   Tobin's q is the market value of the firm relative to the replacement cost of the firm's assets.

agement, reducing grievances (through their "collective voice" function), and so on. These participatory benefits can, however, be countered if unions impede management's ability to adjust to changing economic circumstances or if they impose restrictive practices (such as overstaffing or guaranteed overtime).

In most empirical studies, productivity is defined as either labor productivity or total factor productivity.[35] The union/nonunion productivity differential is typically estimated from *a production function model*. Productivity is explained by the input mix (employment, capital, and hours worked), a vector of observed firm and industry characteristics (for example, industry concentration), a union dummy variable, and other control variables (such as business cycle indicators or the level of union coverage in the industry). The production function approach has a number of problems. First, measured productivity in unionized firms can be higher than in nonunionized firms without implying that unionized firms are more efficient. This is because the wage markup, other things being equal, reduces employment in unionized firms. As a consequence, the marginal product of labor would be higher in unionized firms than in nonunionized ones.[36] Second, unionized firms are likely to change their input mix in response to the wage markup. Hence, the input mix cannot be considered an exogenous determinant of productivity, and a simultaneity bias can develop. A third problem arises because management's role is largely ignored. Since the interaction between management and unions affects productivity levels, ignoring management can give a biased view of the impact of unions (Denny 1997). This problem is more generally related to unobserved heterogeneity and can best be dealt with by estimating productivity growth models instead of productivity level models. With these methodological issues in mind, we now review studies that estimate the productivity level and growth differential. We start with the evidence related to the productivity level differential.

---

35. Typically, value added per employee or per working hour is used to proxy productivity. Only a few studies use physical output. The use of value added rather than physical output tends to overestimate the productivity differentials because of price effects. For example, if the wage markup leads to higher product prices, then productivity will appear to increase without unions having any beneficial impact on output. Total factor productivity takes into account that more than one factor of production is used to produce output. More specifically, total factor productivity growth is defined as the growth of output less the weighted sum of the growth of the relevant inputs, where the weights are given by the shares of each input.

36. This argument assumes that the firm is operating at its labor demand curve rather than entering efficient contracts.

The productivity level differential. Bellman (1992) has surveyed the empirical literature from the United States.[37] His conclusion, based on the evidence from 17 studies, is a qualified one, as there is considerable variation across industries. In those industries in which firms are subject to substantial product market competition, unionized firms have higher productivity levels than nonunionized ones. The quality of industrial relations is also important. The "quality" of industrial relations is proxied by the number of grievances filed, the number of unresolved grievances, the number of strikes and quits, and the use of long-term collective agreements. Firms with high-quality industrial relations are associated with higher productivity levels and higher product quality than firms with low-quality industrial relations.[38] On the other hand, the significantly higher absenteeism among union workers than among nonunion workers can have a negative impact on productivity; some studies find that absenteeism is 30 percent higher among unionized workers than among nonunionized ones (Allen 1984; Katz, Kochan, and Gobeille 1983).

Booth (1995) and Metcalf (1993) have surveyed the evidence from the United Kingdom. Booth tentatively concludes that U.K. unions appear to have a negative impact on the level of productivity, but this conclusion is far from robust. For example, Denny (1997) shows how the productivity effect of unions varies over time. His evidence suggests that British unions had no impact on productivity levels before 1979, but in the Thatcher era in the early 1980s, unions appeared to have a negative impact on productivity. It is noteworthy that the results are affected by how unionism is measured. For example, those studies that use union density as an indicator of unionism find a negative productivity effect. However, studies that use strikes as an indicator tend to find positive or insignificant effects.[39] This suggests that the adverse impact of unions on the productivity level is not due to industrial conflict.

In Japan, unions are enterprise based and concentrated in larger firms, and the attitude of Japanese unions is often viewed as cooperative with management. Hence, Japanese unions seem like an obvious place to look for the "collective voice" effect of unions. Nevertheless, empirical studies

---

37.   See also Addison and Hirsch (1989), Booth (1995: chapter 7), and Filer, Hamermesh, and Rees (1996: chapter 13).

38.   It is not obvious that the number of grievances filed is an indicator of high-quality industrial relations. While a large number of grievances filed can indicate that workers are able to express their dissatisfaction within the firm, it can also indicate that something is wrong in the workplace. It is therefore not surprising that Katz, Kochan, and Gobeille (1983) have found that the number of grievances filed in a union workplace negatively affects productivity.

39.   See Knight (1989) and Moreton (1993).

from Japan find that unions have mixed effects on productivity. Muramatsu (1984) observed that unions had a positive impact on productivity levels for 1978 when technology and labor-quality variables are held constant,[40] while Brunello (1992) found that productivity in unionized firms was 15 percent lower than in similar nonunionized firms. In Germany, unions appear to have no impact on productivity. This may be related to the fact that all German workplaces have work councils that provide the collective voice function of unions, even in nonunionized firms (Schnabel 1991).

Malaysia is the only middle-income economy for which evidence on productivity (level) differentials is available. Standing (1992) uses the value of total sales relative to the total work force to proxy productivity. He finds that unionized firms have higher productivity levels than nonunionized firms and that the positive productivity differential is primarily associated with industrial rather than company unions. While Standing argues that this is prima facie evidence that unions have been associated with dynamic efficiency effects in Malaysia, it is somewhat puzzling why the strongest productivity effects are associated with industrial unions. Although industrial unions typically have shop-level facilities, we would expect that company-based unions would be just as good and perhaps in even a better position than industry-based unions to provide a "voice" and other efficiency-enhancing services.

The productivity growth differential. The U.S. evidence on the union/nonunion productivity growth differential has been reviewed by Booth (1995: chapter 7) and Bellman (1992). Bellman finds that in five out of nine cross-sectional studies and in all time-series studies that he reviewed unions decrease productivity growth. In the remaining four cross-sectional studies, no significant difference was found between unionized and nonunionized firms. While the available evidence indicates that British unions may have a negative impact on productivity levels, the evidence regarding productivity growth is mixed. Some studies, for example, suggest that unionized firms have higher productivity growth than nonunionized firms during the period 1979–84 (Nickell, Wadhawani, and Wall 1989). In the 1980s, many firms derecognized unions and repudiated closed shop arrangements. Gregg, Mashin, and Szymanski (1993) consider how these changes in union arrangements affect the productivity growth differential. While they find no difference between productivity growth in unionized and nonunionized firms between 1984 and 1987, firms that experienced a

---

40.   The difference is about 20 percent. However, since net value added per employee is used as a measure of productivity, the difference may reflect the effects of unions on prices through cost-push.

change in union arrangements between 1987 and 1989 had higher productivity growth than both unionized firms with constant union arrangements and nonunionized firms. These results indicate that the weakening of British unions is one factor that explains the high productivity growth in the 1980s in the United Kingdom (Booth 1995: 208). Finally, Bean and Symons (1989) estimate a reduced form productivity growth equation for 19 OECD countries for the period 1950–80. Their analysis mainly concludes that union density does not have a statistically significant impact on productivity growth.

Unions and Implementation of New Technology

Unions' attitude toward new technology (for example, computers and new machinery) is unclear. On the one hand, unions may resist technological changes because they fear immediate short-run employment losses. On the other hand, they may take a long-run view and welcome new technology that increases productivity and the prospect for future increases in wages.

The available empirical evidence suggests that new technology is adopted as fast in unionized firms as in nonunionized ones and that unions have little impact on technological innovation in firms. Keefe (1992) surveys research on the relationship between unions and technological change in the United States, the United Kingdom, and Canada in the 1980s. He concludes that "unions have no effect on firms' use of advanced manufacturing and microelectronic technologies" and that "in most cases unions welcome technological modernization; sometimes encouraging it, most often accepting it, infrequently opposing it but usually seeking to protect their members" (Keefe 1992: 110–11). Betcherman (1991) reaches a similar conclusion in his study of the impact of unions on technological change in Canada in 1980–85 but observes that unions do have an impact on the way in which technological change is implemented. In particular, he finds that unionized firms were more likely to introduce technological changes than nonunionized firms for cost-cutting or production control reasons. Likewise, Daniels (1987), Latreille (1992), and Machin and Wadhwani (1991) find that unions had a small positive impact on the introduction of new microelectronic equipment in U.K. firms in the mid-1980s. Finally, Standing (1992), in his study of industrial relations in Malaysia, concludes that unions actually stimulate capital, product, and labor process innovations.

Unions, Physical Investments, and R&D

The reviewed evidence on the wage markup and the effect of unions on profitability shows that unions share rents with firms. Besides the static impact on the functional distribution of income, this can have significant dynamic efficiency effects. These arise when firms realize that workers are going to appropriate part of the profits associated with investments in physical capital and R&D. Consequently, a unionized firm can be expected to invest less than a similar firm operating in a competitive labor market because of the resulting "hold-up problem" (Grout 1984; Ulph and Ulph 1990).

A handful of studies have looked into the issue of under-investment by unionized firms, using firm- or industry-level data from the United States and the United Kingdom. For the United States, Bronars and Deere (1986) and Hirsch (1990) and for the United Kingdom, Denny and Nickell (1991) find that unionization has a negative impact on investment in physical capital. For example, Denny and Nickell (1991) find that, holding wages and productivity constant, the rate of investment in firms that recognize a union and have an average manual union density is, on average, 23 percent lower than in other firms. Furthermore, distinguishing between competitive and noncompetitive sectors and taking second round wage effects into account, they find that the net reduction in the investment rate is 13 percent for a competitive, unionized firm but only about 4 percent for a noncompetitive, unionized one.[41] This result is surprising in suggesting that product market competition has an adverse impact on the behavior of unions.

Likewise, the available evidence suggests that unionization can reduce spending on R&D (Acs and Audretsch 1987; Connolly, Hirsch, and Hirschey 1986; Ulph and Ulph 1989). Van Reenen (1993) estimates that firm-level innovations in unionized British manufacturing firms are associated with higher wages for up to seven years. This suggests that unions do share in the surplus from innovation and may explain why the spending on R&D is lower in unionized firms than in nonunionized ones.

Unions, Fringe Benefits, and Health and Safety Regulations

Unions do significantly increase wages. While this can be interpreted as evidence that unionized workers earn substantial rents, Duncan and Strafford (1980) argue that as much as two-fifths of the wage markup is compensation for an inflexible and employer-controlled work environment. In addition to their monthly paycheck, however, unionized workers may be concerned with other issues, such as bonuses, severance pay, health and safety regulations, and paid sick leave.

---

41. The distinction between competitive and noncompetitive industries is based on a workplace survey in which firms are asked to indicate if the market they are operating in (a) is dominated by the main supplier, (b) has only a few comp titors, or (c) has many competitors.

The evidence suggests that workers in unionized firms are more likely to receive these benefits than are workers in nonunionized firms. For instance, in Malaysia, Standing (1992) finds that firms with unions are more likely to provide paid sick leave, retirement benefits, cheap loans, and transportation. Green, Hadjimatheou, and Smail (1985) find that unions increase the likelihood of improved health and safety measures in the United Kingdom. Nakumura, Sato, and Kamiya (1988) find that unions in Japan increase the use of severance pay and the size of the yearly bonus.

Some of these benefits obviously contribute to increasing labor costs in general and turnover costs in particular. On the other hand, cheap loans, free transportation, paid sick leave, and safety regulations may improve worker motivation and pay off in terms of higher productivity. Moreover, to the extent that inadequate safety and health provisions generate a suboptimal allocation of labor, union-sponsored (as well as government-sponsored) safety and health regulations increase not only individual worker's welfare but also aggregate welfare. Maskus, Rutherford, and Selby (1995) consider this issue of disclosure of information in the context of the risk attributes of different jobs. Commodities produced in different sectors use production technologies that expose workers to different levels of physical risks, such as exposure to toxins and industrial accidents. Safety is desirable from the point of view of workers. Therefore, safety has an opportunity cost, and safer jobs pay a lower wage. In an unregulated labor market, workers may be unable to appreciate the dangers inherent in different jobs. As a consequence, firms would not be required to compensate workers fully for the hidden risks involved in their jobs. This would lead to an inefficient allocation of labor across sectors, with too many workers doing jobs that are too dangerous. A labor market reform that induces full disclosure of safety levels would remove this distortion. Maskus, Rutherford, and Selby (1995: table 2) estimate the welfare effects of a labor market reform of this type using a CGE model of the Mexican economy. They find that the well-being of workers would increase by 0.5 percent of baseline GDP per year. Moreover, the real income of the owners of the firms would increase as well because the reform increases the demand for capital for risk-abatement purposes. The total gain is estimated to be 0.6 percent of baseline GDP per year. This is a substantial gain and is of the same order of magnitude as the estimated monopoly cost of unions.

Individual Performance Pay and Seniority

Freeman and Medoff (1984) find that individual performance pay is much more prevalent among nonunionized firms in the United States than among unionized firms by as much as 16 to 23 percentage points.

Similar results are found in Britain. Blanchflower and Oswald (1988) use a questionnaire to identity the factors that influence the level of pay in wage settlements in the private sector in Britain. They find that the most significant difference between unionized and nonunionized firms is that individual performance is important in wage determination only in nonunionized firms.

This can have an adverse effect on productivity if individual performance pay is used as an incentive to increase workers' efforts. However, there are counterarguments. For example, the fact that unions are able to reduce the use of individual performance pay could be seen as evidence that the presence of unions reduces the need for this control instrument. Seniority-based wages can be interpreted as an efficiency wage that is designed to motivate workers to stay with the same firm for a longer period of time. Therefore, unions can increase productivity by extending seniority-based systems to smaller firms.[42]

Unions and Pensions

Evidence from Canada, Malaysia, and the United States shows that unions increase the likelihood that workers are enrolled in pension schemes.[43] As pointed out by Freeman (1985), if union-sponsored pension plans do not replace private saving, national saving can increase. At the macroeconomic level, the implied reduction in the real interest rate will increase investment demand and may even have a (temporary) impact on economic growth.

Conclusion

In chapter 3, we argued that the net cost of unions has three components: the monopoly cost, the participatory benefits, and the rent-seeking cost. To conclude the discussion of the microeconomic effects of unions, we integrate the evidence surveyed in the previous sections to make an overall evaluation of the monopoly costs and the participatory benefits of unions. A detailed summary of the results can be found in the chapter 1. Our examination of the empirical evidence has little to add to our theoretical discussion of unions as rent-seekers (see chapter 3) and so this (potentially important) aspect of union behavior is not subject to separate consideration below.

---

42.   Large firms tend to have seniority-based wage systems largely irrespective of unionization (Brown 1990: 178).

43.   See Freeman (1985), Kupferschmidt and Swidensky (1989), and Standing (1992).

The Monopoly Cost of Unions

The evidence on the wage markup shows that unions everywhere are successful in raising wages for their members and others covered by collective agreements. As pointed out by Rees (1963), this creates a misallocation of resources. However, attempts to quantify the size of this deadweight loss have consistently shown that it is relatively small, no larger than 0.5 percent of GDP per year. It should be kept in mind, however, that these estimates do not include all the potential costs of unions. While they do take into account that the level of employment is likely to be reduced, they do not include the costs associated with a reduction in employment growth, nor do they include rent-seeking costs. The estimates also disregard a number of potential dynamic costs of unionism. First, the evidence reviewed above shows that unions compress the reward to skill accumulation. This, other things being equal, reduces workers' incentives to engage in training and education. Second, the evidence reviewed above also suggests that unions can have an adverse impact on firms' incentive to invest in physical capital and R&D, although there is no evidence that unions reduce the speed at which new technologies are adopted.

Theoretical considerations suggest that firms' exposure to competition from product markets and nonunion labor markets can potentially help to reduce the monopoly cost of unions. Here we have found some evidence to support this view, but it is far from conclusive. First, the measured impact of product market competition on the wage markup is sensitive to the method used to measure the degree of product market competition. When industry concentration indicators are used, the markup is typically found to be relatively small for unionized workers employed in industries with high concentration. Arguably, however, industry concentration is not a good indicator of the competitive situation facing individual firms, and other studies, which use firm-specific indicators of competitive pressure, find that competitive pressure from product markets does reduce the wage markup. In addition, the evidence shows that the adverse impact of unions on profitability is relatively small when firms have little monopoly power in the product market.

There are good theoretical reasons to believe that the monopoly cost is systematically related to the institutional framework in which collective bargaining takes place. The empirical evidence is, however, mixed. Some studies show that the wage markup is small when bargaining is conducted at the firm level rather than at the industry level but the differences are not large, and some studies from the United Kingdom are unable to detect any differences. Nevertheless, it is possible to identify particular aspects of collective bargaining, such as the combination of multiunionism and separate collective bargaining and pre-entry closed shops, that definitely add to the wage markup as well as other aspects, such as post-entry closed shops, that do not.

Participatory Benefits of Unions

We would expect the participatory benefits of unions to show up as productivity differences between unionized and nonunionized firms. The evidence shows that unions have little impact on productivity levels and growth on average. Under special circumstances, however, unions can have a positive impact. In firms where industrial relations are of a "high" quality (in terms of a low number of unsolved grievances, low strike activity, and so on), the presence of unions tend to increase productivity levels. The same is true in firms that are operating in a competitive product market environment. An important source of participatory benefits is a reduction in labor turnover. Here the evidence shows that turnover is significantly lower in unionized firms than elsewhere. The gain associated with this reduction is estimated to be 0.2 to 0.3 percent of GDP. This gain is on the same order of magnitude as the estimated deadweight loss associated with the wage markup. In addition, by making it more profitable for workers to engage in firm-specific training and for firms to fund general training programs, the observed reduction in turnover can explain why union members are more likely to be trained than other workers.

In conclusion, the costs and benefits of unions depend on the economic (and political) environment in which unions and employers interact. It is crucial to keep this in mind when contemplating policy reforms.

5

Empirical Evidence from Macroeconomic Studies

The labor market has important influences on the functioning of the macroeconomy. This suggests that different institutional approaches to collective bargaining can lead to very different macroeconomic outcomes, and that some institutional arrangements might be more appropriate to achieve desirable outcomes than others. A central idea is that collective bargaining facilitates coordination. Coordination can take make forms. For example, the Japanese system of wage setting is decentralized (firm based) but coordinated in the sense that it follows company rules based on seniority rather than individual contracting. The Netherlands and Germany also have coordinated systems through strong employer organizations, coordination between giant companies or across industries, and between unions. Coordination in France is through the government in the form of public services, utilities, and large nationalized industries. In Italy, there is informal employer coordination (via the big firms and regional employers' associations) and between some union confederations. Finally, centralized employers' organizations as well as centralized union confederations have dominated Sweden and more generally Scandinavian labor markets. It is clear from these examples that the specific institutions and the extent to which pay and work conditions are determined by collective agreements as oppose to individual contracts differ quite a lot across the OECD. These differences combined with the observed differences in macroeconomic performance (primarily in terms of unemployment and inflation) between the OECD countries over the last 30 years has spurred a large literature that tries to explain cross-country variation in economic performance by cross-country differences in labor market institutions. The purpose of this chapter is to examine this literature in detail and ask what can be learned about the impact of collective bargaining on macroeconomic performance from it.

Conceptual Issues

From a normative perspective, we would like to design labor market institutions that in some sense maximize social welfare subject to economic and non-economic constraints (where noneconomic constraints may include geographical, historical, cultural, political, social, and religious ones):

Max (welfare)
Subject to (constraints)

Since welfare is not observed, economists typically think of maximizing some aggregate economic outcome that captures aspects of social welfare, such as the output level or employment. The aggregate outcome (Y) relates to the n suboutcomes (y_i) in some general form:

(1) $Y = f(y_1, y_2, ..., y_n)$.

Although conceptually clear, the measurement of the aggregate economic outcome requires that we know how to aggregate as well as measure the suboutcomes. One way to solve the aggregation problem is to impose some assumption such as

(2) $Y = y_1 + y_2 + ... + y_n$.

There is, however, no reason why suboutcomes should be given equal importance (or measured in the same units). They could be given different weights. Unfortunately, the weights usually have to be chosen arbitrarily, and in any case it is also possible that a multiplicative rather than an additive relationship is more appropriate. Mainly due to all these difficulties, the prevalent approach in the literature is to assess the impact of the institutional framework of collective bargaining on economic performance by looking at one sub-outcome as measured by an economic indicator at the time, and then try to aggregate (often implicitly) the suboutcomes in a meaningful way.

Measuring Labor Market Institutions and Economic Performance

To evaluate the impact of collective bargaining on macroeconomic performance in a comparative context, aspects of the relevant labor market institutions have to be measured empirically and examined against indicators of macroeconomic performance. Measuring differences in labor market institutions over time and space in a consistent and meaningful way is perhaps the greatest obstacle for comparative study, and we shall devote considerable attention to this issue in what follows.

Institutional Indicators

The comparative literature attempts to measure cross-country differences in labor market institutions by looking at a few crude indicators. The simplest way to capture the importance of collective bargaining in an economy is to measure the proportion of the economy in which pay and employment conditions are determined by collective bargaining between employers and employees rather than by individual contracts. In practice, *union density* and *bargaining coverage* are used to capture this aspect of collective bargaining (see table 5-1). These two indicators go some way in measuring the "importance" of collective agreements as opposed to individual contracts, but they can hardly be seen as indicators of union power. In particular, it should be kept in mind that there can be substantial spillover effects from unionized/covered sectors to nonunionized/uncovered sectors that are not captured by the two indicators. For instance, firms in noncovered sectors may set wages at the collectively agreed level to avoid being subject to other effects of unionization or to motivate their workers who may be concerned about relative wages (Mazumdar 1993; Pencavel 1991).

Table 5-2 shows data on union density and bargaining coverage for 19 OECD countries for the period 1970–94. Average union density increased from 43 percent to 47 percent during the 1970s but declined to 40 percent during the 1980s and 1990s. However, the average hides a lot of variation. Some countries, such as Japan, the Netherlands, the United Kingdom, and the United States, have experienced a significant reduction in union density. Other countries, such as Finland and Sweden, have encountered

Table 5-1. Definitions of Union Density and Bargaining Coverage

Term	Definition
Union density	The number of workers who are members of a union, as a percentage of all workers, unionized and nonunionized.
Bargaining coverage	The number of workers, unionized or not, whose pay and employment conditions are determined by a collective agreement, as a percentage of all workers, unionized and nonunionized.

Note: Depending on the study, the term "all workers" refers to all wage and salary workers (employees) or total labor force (employees plus self-employed, family workers, and so on).

Source: OECD (1997).

Table 5-2.   Union Density and Bargaining Coverage in Selected OECD Countries

Country	Union density			Bargaining coverage		
	1970	1980	1994	1980	1990	1994
Australia	50	48	41	88	80	80
Austria	62	56	42	98	98	98
Belgium	46	56	54	90	90	90
Canada	31	36	38	37	38	38
Denmark[a]	60	76	76	69	69	69
Finland	51	70	81	95	95	95
France	22	18	9	85	92	95
Germany	33	36	29	91	90	92
Italy	36	49	39	85	83	82
Japan[a]	35	31	24	28	23	21
Netherlands	38	35	26	76	71	81
New Zealand	—	56	30	67	67	31
Norway	51	57	58	75	75	74
Portugal	61	61	32	70	79	71
Spain	27	19	19	76	76	78
Sweden[a]	68	80	91	86	86	89
Switzerland	30	31	27	53	53	50
United Kingdom	45	50	34	70	47	47
United States	23	22	16	26	18	18
Average	43	47	40	72	70	68

— Not available.

a. In three cases (Denmark, Japan, and Sweden), bargaining coverage is less than union density. This difference can arise if some workers are members of a union for reasons other than to get the collectively agreed wage. In Japan, about 30 percent of people belonging to a union were not covered by collective agreements. The difference in Denmark and Sweden can arise because professional white-collar workers in the private sector belong to the union but are able to get a better individual wage deal than the collectively agreed one. Alternatively, the difference can reflect differences in the construction of the two numbers (see OECD 1997: annex 3.a).

Source: Freeman (1988a) and OECD (1997: table 3.3).

a significant increase in union density over the three decades. Also, the cross-country variation is significant. Countries such as France, Spain, and the United States have very low union density rates (less than 30 percent). On the other hand, the Scandinavian countries have very high rates (all above 50 percent and some around 80 percent). Bargaining coverage is, on average, much higher than union density and was relatively constant around 70 percent during the period. While high union density leads to high coverage of collective bargaining, table 5-2 shows that the converse is not true. Countries such as France and Spain have very low union density, yet the coverage of collective agreements is very high. The difference between union density and the coverage of collective bargaining is largely attributed to mandatory extensions of collective agreements to nonunionized sectors (OECD 1994).

Table 5-3 shows data on union density in a selection of developing countries and newly industrialized countries. These are calculated as the number of unionized workers as a percentage of the nonagricultural work force and refer to the 1980s. While these figures may not be directly

Table 5-3.   Union Density in Selected Developing Countries and Newly Industrialized Countries in the 1980s

Country	Union density
Guatemala	9
Guyana	32
Haiti	2
Honduras	20
Hong Kong (China)	19
India	9
Jamaica	24
Korea, Republic of	24
Malaysia	14
Mexico	29
Nicaragua	35
Panama	16
Paraguay	4
Peru	29
St. Kitts and Nevis	34
St. Lucia	20
St. Vincent and Grenadine	12
Singapore	17
Suriname	42
Taiwan (China)	33
Thailand	6
Trinidad and Tobago	28
Uruguay	15
Venezuela	31
Average	21

Note: Union density is typically defined as the number of organized workers as a percentage of the nonagricultural work force.
Source: Arudsothy and Littler (1993), Frenkel (1993: table 11.1), and Rama (1995).

comparable to those of the OECD, it is nevertheless interesting to notice that union density in the average developing country is only half as large as in the average OECD country (21 percent compared to 40 percent).

Another aspect of collective bargaining emphasized by comparative studies is *bargaining coordination*. This is much harder to measure empirically than union density and bargaining coverage, and one has to make subjective judgments (for example, is Sweden more "coordinated" than Germany?). The literature attempts to measure six (related) aspects of bargaining coordination in different countries. These are summarized in table 5-4 and have been discussed already in chapter 3. In practice, the relevant OECD countries are ranked or classified based on an assessment of the degree of bargaining coordination in each country at a given point in time.[1] While some researchers focus on particular aspects in their assessment, most use a cluster of different aspects of bargaining coordination to construct the ranking or classification.

Table 5-5 characterizes the 28 indicators of bargaining coordination used in the studies surveyed here. Each row provides information on how a particular indicator has been constructed. The first column cites the source of the study that constructed the indicator. The second column indicates which aspects of bargaining coordination the study emphasized.[2] Each of the indicators is then given a code name for mnemonic purposes (column 3). The subsequent columns are labeled A to G. They refer to the aspects of coordination, presented in table 5-4, that were used to construct the indicators in each individual study. The last two columns refer, respectively, to the period for which the characterization of bargaining coordination applies (the reference period) and to whether the study developed its own indicator of bargaining coordination or used or updated an existing one.

A few remarks about the indicators of bargaining coordination are appropriate. First, the table includes a number of indexes that refer to corporatism. These indexes are derived from the economic literature and, except for Tarantelli (1986), focus on centralization, concentration, and informal coordination rather than on social partnership and other political aspects. A large political science literature looks into the political aspects of corporatism in much more detail, but it is not reviewed here (Lijphard and Crepaz 1991). Second, most of the indicators combine a cluster of different aspects of bargaining coordination and are therefore

---

1.   Some studies construct an index rather than a ranking. To do so, each country is given a score on different dimensions of bargaining coordination, and the scores are added to an overall score. By doing so, it is implicitly assumed that the degree of coordination can be measured on a cardinal scale. This, of course, is a dubious assumption.

2.   A detailed discussion of each of the indicators included in the survey can be found in appendix 1.

Table 5-4.   Aspects of Bargaining Coordination

Aspect	Definition
A. Union centralization	Union centralization is the capacity of the national union confederation to influence wage levels and patterns across the economy.
B. Union concentration	Union concentration is high if "few" unions at the relevant level of bargaining are representing workers.
C. Employer centralization	Employer centralization is the capacity of the national employers' confederation to influence wage levels and patterns across the economy.
D. Level of bargaining	Collective bargaining takes place at different levels: the firm level, the industry level, and the regional/national level.
E. Informal coordination	Informal coordination includes (a) informal consultations at the industry, regional, or national level among unions and firms, and (b) pattern bargaining (an agreement in a dominant sector mimicked by others).
F. Corporatism	Corporatism is a combination of (a) high union density and bargaining coverage and high degree of union and employer centralization/concentration and (b) social partnership between national workers' and employers' organizations and the government.
G. Other aspects[a]	This include different types of dispute resolution procedures, the proportion of unionized workers employed in sectors that are subject to international competition, and union density.

a. Cameron (1984) includes union density in his "index of organization power of labor." Crouch (1990) includes the proportion of unionized workers employed in sectors that are subject to international competition in his "index of power of exposed-sector unions." Taranetelli (1986) includes information about differences in dispute settlement mechanisms in his "index of neo-corporatism."

Source: Authors.

highly correlated.[3] This makes it difficult to isolate empirically the effects of individual aspects of bargaining coordination on macroeconomic performance. Third, although researchers in this area are familiar with the details of bargaining systems in many different countries and some

---

3.   OECD (1997: table 3.4) estimates the correlation between OECD1997-1/2 and S1990-1, CD1988, BS1985, S1981, C1984, LNJ1991-1/2 and T1986, respectively, to be in the range of 0.67–0.84. See also table 5-19.

Table 5-5. Characterization of 28 Indicators of Bargaining Coordination

Source/study	Indicator gives emphasis on:	Indicator code	A	B	C	D	E	F	G	Reference period	Index used
Dowrick (1993)	Coordination	D1993-2	X	(X)	(X)	X	X			1960s, 1970s, and 1980s	C1990-1, CD1988, S1990
Layard, Nickell, and Jackman (1991)	Employee coordination	LNJ1991-1	X	X		X	X			1980s	Own
Layard, Nickell, and Jackman (1991)	Employer coordination	LNJ1991-2	X		X	X	X			1980s	Own
Layard, Nickell, and Jackman (1991)	Employer and employee coordination	LNJ1991-1/2	X	X	X	X	X			1980s	LNJ1991-1 LNJ1991-2
OECD (1997)	Coordination	OECD1997-2	X		X		X			1980, 1990, and 1994	Own
OECD (1997)	Centralization and informal coordination	OECD1991-3	X		X	X	X			1980, 1990, and 1994	OECD1997-1 and OECD1997-2
Soskice (1990)	Economy-wide coordination	S1990	X		X	X	X			1985–90	Own
Blau and Kahn (1996)	Centralization	BK1996	X	X	X	X			Union density	1970s 1980s	BS1985 CD1988 C1984-1 Others
Bleaney (1996)	Corporatism and centralization	B1996	X	X	X					1970s 1980s	BS1985 CD1988
Heitger (1987)	Corporatism	H1987	X	X	X					1970s	BS1985

(table continues on following page)

Table 5-5 continued

Source/study	Indicator gives emphasis on:	Indicator code	A	B	C	D	E	F	G	Reference period	Index used
Bruno and Sacks (1985)	Corporatism	BS1985	X	X	X					1970s	Crouch (1985)
Calmfors and Drifill (1988)	Centralization	CD1988	X	X	X	X				1980s	Own
Cameron (1984)	Organizational power of labor	C1984-1	X	X					Union density	1965–80	Own
Cameron (1984)	Union centralization	C1984-2	X							1965–80	Own
Cameron (1984)	Union concentration	C1984-3		X						1965–80	Own
Crouch (1985)	Neocorporatism	C1985	X							1970s	Own
Crouch (1990)	Labor movement centralization	C1990	X			X				1960s, 1970s, and 1980s	Own
Dowrick (1993)	Centralization	D1993-1	X	(X)	(X)	X				1960s, 1970s, and 1980s	CD1988, C1990-1
Lange and Garrett (1985)	Organizational power of labor	GL1985	X	X						1965–80	C1984
McCallum (1986)	Corporatism	MC1986	X	X	X					1970s	Crouch (1985)
Newell and Symons (1987)	Corporatism	NS1987	X	X	X					1955–83	Own
OECD (1997)	Bargaining centralization	OECD1997-1				X				1980, 1990, and 1994	OECD (1994)
Schmitter (1981)	Corporatism	S1981-1	X	X						1960s 1970s	Own
Schmitter (1981)	Union centralization	S1981-2	X							1960s 1970s	Own
Schmitter (1981)	Union concentration	S1981-3		X						1960s 1970s	Own

(table continues on following page)

Table 5-5 continued

Source/study	Indicator gives emphasis on:	Indicator code	A	B	C	D	E	F	G	Reference period	Index used
Soskice (1990)	Wage drift	S1990-2	X							1985–90	Own
Taranetelli (1986)	Neocorporatism	T1986	X		X	X		X	Dispute settlement	1970s	Own
Crouch (1990)	Power of unions in trade-exposed sectors	C1990-2							Foreign competition	1960s, 1970s, and 1980s	Own

Note: A = union centralization, B = union concentration, C = employer centralization, D = the level of bargaining, E = informal coordination among employees and employers, F = corporatism/social partnership, and G = other aspects. "Reference period" is the time period for which a particular indicator is descriptive. "Index used" refers to whether the study developed its own indicator of coordination or used or updated an existing one.

Source: Authors.

try to use hard evidence to construct their indicator (see, for example, Cameron 1984), the resulting rankings of countries involve a large element of subjectivity. Not surprisingly, researchers often strongly disagree on the ranking of particular countries (see, for example, the discussion in Soskice [1990] of Calmfors and Driffill [1988]). Fourth, even in highly centralized bargaining systems, collective bargaining takes place at many different levels. As discussed in chapter 3, under multilevel bargaining, the macroeconomic impact of collective bargaining depends on the extent to which wage drift can be controlled. This aspect is largely ignored in the construction of the indexes listed in table 5-5—a fact that may bias the empirical investigation.

Table 5-6 presents country rankings based on four indicators of bargaining coordination. The first column refers to the ranking of Calmfors and Driffill (1988), the second to Soskice (1990), and the last two sets of columns to OECD (1997). These four rankings are indicative of the variation in the degree of bargaining coordination that arises from using

Table 5-6. Country Rankings Based on Alternative Valuations of Bargaining Coordination

Country	S1990-1 1980s	CD1988 1985–90	OECD1997-1 1980	1990	1994	OECD1997-2 1980	1990	1994
Australia	—	10	3	1	14	7	5	15
Austria	2	1	3	1	1	1	1	1
Belgium	—	8	3	1	1	10	10	9
Canada	—	17	17	17	16	18	17	16
Denmark	—	4	3	8	5	4	5	6
Finland	—	5	2	4	4	7	5	6
France	9	11	8	8	5	13	10	9
Germany	6	6	8	8	5	1	1	1
Italy	8	13	15	14	5	15	15	4
Japan	1	14	17	17	16	1	1	1
Netherlands	7	7	8	8	5	10	10	9
New Zealand	—	9	8	16	16	15	17	16
Norway	4	2	8	1	1	4	4	4
Portugal	—	—	15	1	5	13	10	9
Spain	—	—	3	8	5	10	10	9
Sweden	5	3	1	1	5	4	5	9
Switzerland	3	15	8	8	5	7	5	6
United Kingdom	10	12	8	14	14	15	16	16
United States	11	16	17	17	16	18	17	16

— Not available.

Note: The codes refer to table 5-5. A *low* rank is an indication of a *high* degree of bargaining coordination.

Source: Calmfors and Driffill (1988), Soskice (1990), and OECD (1997).

different indicators (see appendix 1 for information on other rankings). Two of the indicators, CD1988 and OECD1997-1, relate to the formal aspects of bargaining coordination such as centralization of collective bargaining and the level of bargaining only. While S1990-1 and OECD1997-2 take the formal aspects into account, they also incorporate the informal aspects of bargaining coordination. Although the correlation between the rankings is high, a detailed comparison of the rankings reveals a number of interesting differences.[4] First, some countries such as Austria, Norway, and Sweden are consistently judged to have highly coordinated bargaining systems. Other countries such as Canada, the United Kingdom, and the United States are consistently classified as having uncoordinated bargaining systems. Second, it makes a considerable difference whether or not informal coordination is taken into account. Comparing S1990-1 and OECD1997-2, which do take informal coordination into account, with CD1988 and OECD1997-1, which do not, we see that Japan switches from being among the most coordinated countries in the sample to being among the least coordinated ones. Other countries, such as Belgium, become less coordinated, relatively speaking, when informal bargaining coordination is taken into account. Third, it is evident from the two OECD rankings that bargaining institutions in some countries have changed over time. For instance, Australia, New Zealand, and the United Kingdom have become less coordinated and less centralized between 1980 and 1994, whereas Italy and Portugal have moved in the opposite direction. However, the positions of other countries in the sample have not changed dramatically.

Macroeconomic Performance Indicators

Table 5-7 summarizes the indicators of economic performance commonly used in the literature. Some studies have simultaneously tried to measure different aspects of economic performance. This is done by combining different indicators (as those defined in table 5-7) to produce a performance index. The four most commonly used performance indexes are defined in table 5-8. Finally, rather than focusing on economic outcomes, as measured by individual indicators or indexes, some studies address the issue of labor market flexibility. Labor market flexibility is measured by real wage flexibility, adjustment speed to wage shocks,

---

4.   OECD (1997: table 3.4) estimates the correlation between OECD1997-1/2 and S1990-1, CD1988, BS1985, S1981, C1984, LNJ1991-1/2 and T1986, respectively, to be in the range of 0.67–0.84. See also table 5-19.

Table 5-7. Definitions of Macroeconomic Performance Indicators

Performance indicator	Definition [a]
Employment rate[b]	The employed as a percentage of the labor force.
Unemployment rate[b]	The unemployed as a percentage of the labor force.
Labor supply	Employment/population ratios (working age population, males aged 25–54) or total labor supply (average annual hours worked per employee times employment divided *by* potential working hours per year per worker (2080) times the number of people of working age).
Inflation	The rate of change in the consumer price index or the GDP deflator.
Compensation growth	Growth in real compensation of workers in manufacturing.
Earnings inequality	Percentile difference (such as the 1st to the 9th percentile) of individual wages in the private sector.
Wage dispersion	Coefficient of variation of cross-industry wages.
Productivity growth	Growth in labor or total factor productivity.
Economic growth	Real GDP growth adjusted for differences in purchasing power.

a. The performance indicators are either in levels (typically decade averages) or in changes (typically between decades).

b. Although conceptually these two variables are closely related, in practice they can vary significantly, mainly because unemployment is difficult to measure.

Source: Authors.

Table 5-8. Performance Indexes

Index	Definition
Okun's index	The sum of the unemployment rate and inflation.
Open economy index	The sum of the unemployment rate and current account deficit as a percentage of GDP.
Job quality index	The difference between the employment rate and wage dispersion (coefficient of variation).
Growth/inflation index	The sum of the slowdown in real GNP growth per capita and the rise in inflation between two periods.

Note: The open economy index is also known as the "alternative performance index" (see Calmfors and Driffill 1988).

Source: See Bruno and Sacks (1985), Calmfors and Driffill (1988), and Rowthorn (1992a,b).

unemployment persistence, and how quickly unemployed workers find new jobs. These variables are derived from estimating econometric models of the labor market and are summarized in table 5-9.

Estimation Methodology

The econometric issues involved in estimating the impact on collective bargaining on macroeconomic performance are similar to those arising in other comparative studies of cross-country data. Without going into many of the more technical details, we shall briefly summarize a few methodological points that arise in this context.

The starting point is indicators of collective bargaining and macroeconomic performance for a set of countries. Armed with these the relationship between the two can be represented by the following set of equations:

$$(3) \qquad y_{i,t} = g_{i,t} (z_{i,t}, x_{i,t}, e_{i,t}),$$

where subscript i refers to a particular country and subscript t refers to a particular point in time. $y_{i,t}$ is a vector of (observed) performance indicators (such as the unemployment rate or inflation), $z_{i,t}$ is a vector of institutional indicators (such as union density, bargaining coverage, or bargaining coordination), $x_{i,t}$ is a vector of economic, political, and socioeconomic control variables, and $e_{i,t}$ is a disturbance term. The function $g_{i,t}$ is in principle unrestricted, that is, it may be nonlinear and nonmonotonic.

Table 5-9.   Labor Market Flexibility Indicators

Indicator	Definition
Aggregate real wage flexibility	The responsiveness of the real wage to activity (unemployment).
Hysteresis	Persistence of unemployment shocks, that is, the extent to which high unemployment yesterday causes high unemployment today.
Adjustment speed	The mean adjustment speed of employment to a real wage shock.
Search effectiveness	Number of job vacancies at a given level of unemployment.

Source: Alogoskoufis and Manning (1988); Bean, Layard, and Nickell (1986); Jackman, Pissarides, and Savouri (1990); Layard, Nickell, and Jackman (1991); McCallum (1986); Newell and Symons (1987); and Scarpetta (1996).

Broadly speaking, equation 3 has been estimated in three different ways in the literature. The simplest approach is the correlation approach,[5] which estimates the relationship between two particular indicators as a simple correlation using cross-country data. This approach is obviously very crude. The regression approach[6] uses multiple regression analysis to estimate equation 3, thereby attempting to isolate the impact of a particular institutional indicator from that of other determinants. The two-step regression approach[7] is a more sophisticated version of the regression approach. In the first step, an economic model (such as a system of wage and price equations) is econometrically estimated for each country using time-series data. The results are used to obtain estimated indicators of labor market flexibility (such as real wage flexibility and search effectiveness). In the second step, the relationship (if any) between the estimated indicators and bargaining coordination, union density, and bargaining coverage is analyzed.[8]

Irrespective of the estimation approach, drawing an inference about the relationship between collective bargaining and macroeconomic performance is a challenge. First, the data material is limited and a few outliers can significantly influence the results. Most studies are based on a sample of 10 to 20 observations from OECD countries at a given point in time. Only a few (Dowrick 1993, Heitger 1987, OECD 1997) constructs pooled time-series/cross-country data. This increases the number of observations to about 60 and makes it possible to take unobserved country effects into account. Second, industrial relations *do* change over time but only slowly in response to political and economic conditions.[9] This raises the question of simultaneity biases, as in the long run the

---

5.   See, for example, Calmfors and Driffill (1988) and Bruno and Sacks (1985).

6.   See, for example, Dowrick (1993) and Nickell and Layard (1999).

7.   See, for example, Layard, Nickell, and Jackman (1991) and Scarpetta (1996).

8.   One problem with this approach is that the indicators of bargaining coordination are being telescoped from one period into other periods (Golden 1993). This is, of course, also the case with the correlation and the one-step regression approach, but the problem is more striking with the two-step regression approach than with the others because the time dimension is more apparent.

9.   It is obvious from the experience of New Zealand and the United Kingdom that labor reforms can significantly change the institutional framework of collective bargaining. However, changing economic conditions may have the same effect. For instance, centralized collective bargaining or even social partnership may, in some countries, have been a reasonable way to deal with the major supply side shocks of the 1970s, whereas more decentralized bargaining structures are better able to accommodate the challenge of globalization in the 1990s. Therefore, the tendency to decentralize collective bargaining in some OECD countries (such as Sweden and Denmark) can be seen as an endogenous response to changing economic conditions, in particular changing industry structures.

pressure from emerging economic conditions can call for a reconsideration of the institutional framework. The literature, on the whole, ignores this feedback and assumes that institutional factors affect economic indicators and not vice versa.[10] It is clear, therefore, that one should be careful not to read too much into the empirical results. To reflect this, we focus on the qualitative impact (positive or negative), if any, of collective bargaining on economic performance[11] and stress that cross-country analysis can tell us little about the underlying causal relationship. At best, the analysis can identify empirical regularities that could be made subject to further theoretical or empirical research. With this in mind, we now turn to the evidence.

Union Density and Bargaining Coverage

The relationship between union density and bargaining coverage and a variety of economic performance indicators has been examined extensively (Bean, Layard, and Nickell 1986; Freeman 1988a; Jackman 1993; Layard, Nickell, and Jackman 1991; Nickell 1997; Nickell and Layard 1999; OECD 1997; Scarpetta 1996;). From a theoretical perspective, the impact of union density on economic performance is unclear. Union density determines the number of unionized workers that can be called upon to strike and thereby is a proxy for the bargaining power of unions. In countries with high union density, unions are more likely to succeed in pushing up (union) wages, leading to less employment, more unemployment, and inflation. The negative impact of unionization on economic performance may, however, be reduced if unions participate in productivity-enhancing activities (by giving voice to dissatisfied workers) at the firm level (see the discussion in chapter 3). If these effects are significant, firms may be able to accommodate the wage demands without any significant adverse effects on employment and inflation.

In table 5-10, we summarize the findings of the studies that have investigated the relationship between union density and economic performance. In column one, we give the name of the study and indicate the time period that it covers. In column two, we list the economic performance indicator(s) under investigation. In column three, we indicate to what extent attempts have been made to control for other aspects of collective bargaining than union density (in particular, bargaining coverage and bargaining coordination) and cross-country differences

---

10.   An exception is OECD (1997). They report that the "causality" runs from bargaining institutions to economic performance.

11.   We use the 10 percent level to judge the statistical significance of the estimated effects.

Table 5-10. Union Density and Economic Performance in the OECD Countries: A Summary of Relevant Studies

Study and years	Performance indicator	Control variables	Estimation approach	Result
OECD (1997) 1980–94	Unemployment rate Inflation Employment rate Real earnings growth Earnings inequality	Bargaining coverage OECD 1997-3	Regression approach with pooled cross-country data set	Union density increases the employment rate but has no effect on the unemployment rate, inflation, and real earnings growth. Union density reduces earnings inequality.
OECD (1997) 1980–94	Unemployment rate Inflation Employment rate Real earnings growth Earnings inequality	No control variables	Correlation approach; three points in time: 1980, 1990, and 1994	Union density reduces earnings inequality in 1990 and 1994. Weak indication of a positive relationship between union density and the employment rate and a negative relationship between union density and real earnings growth in 1980 but not in other years.
Freeman (1988a) 1979–85	Unemployment rate Employment rate Compensation	C1985 Wage dispersion Others	Regression approach with cross-country data	Union density has no effect on the unemployment rate, the employment rate, and compensation.
Scarpetta (1996) 1983–93	Unemployment rate	CD1988 LNJ1991-1 LNJ1991-2	Regression approach with cross-country data	Union density increases unemployment, in particular youth and long-term unemployment, but no control for bargaining coverage is made.
Nickell and Layard (1999), 1983–88, 1989–94	Unemployment Labor supply Productivity growth	LNJ1991-1 LNJ1991-2 Bargaining coverage Others	Regression approach with cross-country data	Union density increases total unemployment but has no separate effect on short- and long-term unemployment. Union density has no effect on labor supply and productivity growth.

(table continues on following page)

Table 5-10 continued

Study and years	Performance indicator	Control variables	Estimation approach	Result
Bean, Layard, and Nickell (1986), 1956–85	Adjustment speed Real wage flexibility	BS1985	Two-step regression approach	Union density has no effect on either adjustment speed (to wage shocks) or real wage flexibility.
Layard, Nickell, and Jackman(1991), 1980–94	Real wage flexibility	CD1988 LNJ1991-1 LNJ1991-2 T1986 Others	Two-step regression approach	Union density has no effect on real wage flexibility.
Scarpetta (1996), 1970–93	Hysteresis in unemployment	CD1988 LNJ1991-1 LNJ1991-2	Two-step regression approach	Union density increases unemployment persistence, but no control for bargaining coverage is made.

Note: For more information on the indicators of bargaining coordination in column three, see table 5-5.
Source: Authors.

in economic and political structures. In column four, we indicate the estimation approach used to analyze the relationship. Finally, in column five, we summarize the main results of the study.

Union density per se (for a given level of bargaining coverage and a given level of bargaining coordination) appears to have little or no impact on comparative labor market performance measured by the unemployment rate, inflation, the employment rate, real earnings growth, the level of compensation, labor supply, adjustment speed to wage shocks, real wage flexibility, and labor and total factor productivity.[12] Whereas this can be taken as evidence that, in aggregate, the monopoly behavior of unions in the OECD area is counteracted by collective voice effects, other explanations are also possible. There is, however, one significant exception to the general result that the association between union density and economic performance is weak; high union density is associated with a compression of the wage distribution and a reduction of earnings inequality. This confirms the evidence from the individual-level data discussed in chapter 4, and may be related to egalitarian wage objectives. Finally, high union density may be associated with hysteresis, but Scarpetta (1996), who investigates this issue, does not control for bargaining coverage, and the union density variable may be picking up the effect of bargaining coverage.

The picture looks quite different when we consider the association between union density and economic performance in developing countries. Evidence from Latin America, the Caribbean, and Southeast Asia (Fields and Wan 1989; McGuire 1996; Rama 1995) suggests that union density has a *negative* impact on output and employment growth. Rama (1997b) argues that the difference between the impact of union density in developing and industrial countries is caused by differences in the general economic and political environments of the two groups of countries. In other words, the adverse effect of unions in developing countries is caused not so much by what unions do as by the context in which they are doing it. If unions operate in an environment of generally ill-designed labor and product market regulation in which rent-seeking is a profitable business (also for unions), it is no wonder that the correlation between union density and economic performance is negative. Likewise, if unions operate in the context of an unstable political environment, the incentive to "invest" in real wage restraint in exchange for expected future returns is low, and union militancy, therefore, should come as no surprise. In addition, it could be argued that

---

12.   Blanchflower (1996b), who uses country-specific microeconomic data to analyze OECD countries, comes up with similar results.

the relative lack of bargaining coordination causes union density to have a substantial negative impact on economic performance in the average developing country. In contrast, in the average OECD country, bargaining coordination can offset the adverse impact of high union density. We return to this issue in more detail below.

While union density relates to the number of unionized workers, bargaining coverage relates to the total number of workers whose wage and employment conditions are determined by collective agreements. In table 5-11, we review the studies that have investigated the association between bargaining coverage and macroeconomic performance. The layout of this table is similar to that of table 5-10. After controlling for union density and bargaining coordination, countries with high bargaining coverage (such as Austria, Finland, and France), other things being equal, experience higher unemployment rates, lower employment rates, and more inflation than countries with low bargaining coverage (such as Canada, Japan, and the United States). Moreover, high bargaining coverage seems to increase the supply of labor but has no effect on labor and total factor productivity (Nickell and Layard 1999). Finally, high bargaining coverage is associated with higher real earnings growth and a reduction in earnings inequality.

These findings suggest that an increase in coverage at a given level of union density has a greater impact on economic performance than an increase in density at a given level of coverage. One explanation of this result is as follows. In those parts of the economy to which bargaining results are extended, only the monopoly effect of unions is present. The economic effects of the wage markup, therefore, are not compensated for by worker/management cooperation or other institutional factors that could lead to productivity gains. On average, bargaining coverage can thus affect unemployment, employment, and inflation adversely, whereas the impact of unionization per se can be less significant.

Bargaining Coordination and Comparative Economic Performance: The Big Picture

We have identified 25 comparative, cross-country studies that have examined the relationship between bargaining coordination and economic performance in subsets of OECD countries during the past 30 years.[13]

---

13.   The studies are Bean (1994), Blau and Kahn (1996), Bleaney (1996), Bruno and Sachs (1985), Calmfors and Driffill (1988), Cameron (1984), Crouch (1985, 1990), Dowrick (1993), Freeman (1988a), Golden (1993), Heitger (1987), Jackman (1993), McCallum (1983, 1986), Nickell (1997), Nickell and Layard (1999), OECD (1988, 1997), Rowthorn (1992a, b), Scarpetta (1996), Soskice (1990), Tarantelli (1986), and Zweimuller and Barth (1994).

Table 5-11. Bargaining Coverage and Economic Performance: A Summary of Relevant Studies

Study and years	Performance indicator	Control variables	Estimation approach	Result
OECD (1997) 1980–94	Unemployment rate Inflation Employment rate Real earnings growth Earnings inequality	Union density OECD 1997-3	Regression approach with pooled cross-country data set	Bargaining coverage increases unemployment, inflation, and real earnings growth and reduces the employment rate and earnings inequality.
OECD (1997) 1980–94	Unemployment rate Inflation Employment rate Real earnings growth Earnings inequality	No control variables	Correlation approach at three points in time: 1980, 1990, and 1994	Bargaining coverage increases unemployment only in 1994, reduces the employment rate only in 1990 and 1994, and reduces earnings inequality in 1994. Otherwise it has no impact on economic performance.
Jackman (1993) 1983–88	Unemployment rate	LNJ1991-1 LNJ1991-2 Others	Regression approach with cross-country data	Bargaining coverage increases unemployment.
Nickell and Layard (1999), Nickell (1997), 1989–94	Unemployment rate Labor supply Productivity growth	LNJ1991-1 LNJ1991-2 Union density Others	Regression approach with cross-country data	Bargaining coverage increases both short- and long-term unemployment and labor supply but has no effect on productivity growth.

Note: For more information on the indicators of bargaining coordination in column three, see table 5-5.
Source: Authors.

The literature has focused on two hypotheses, which we discussed in detail in chapter 3:

> **Hypothesis 1.** Coordinated collective bargaining leads to better economic outcomes compared to semicoordinated collective bargaining, which, in turn, performs better than uncoordinated collective bargaining.
>
> **Hypothesis 2.** (The hump hypothesis) Semicoordinated collective bargaining leads to worse economic outcomes than both coordinated and uncoordinated collective bargaining.[14]

The two hypotheses are illustrated in figure 5-1. Hypothesis 1 is shown as curve C and hypothesis 2—the hump hypothesis associated with Calmfors and Driffill (1988)—as curve A. Curve B shows a third possibility.

To structure the discussion of the evidence, we divide the 25 studies into 125 substudies. A substudy (that is, the unit of analysis) is defined as a relationship between a specific indicator of bargaining coordination (defined in table 5-5) vis-à-vis a specific economic indicator (defined in table 5-7 or table 5-8). All the substudies are shown in

Figure 5-1.   Economic Performance and Bargaining

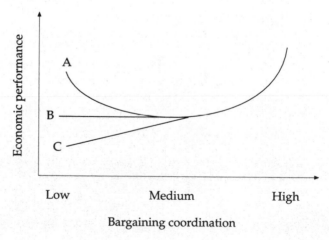

Source: Authors.

---

14.   For example, if semicoordinated schemes are poor performers, then they will have a U-shaped relationship with employment rates and a hump-shaped relationship with unemployment.

appendix 2.[15] Before we proceed, some remarks about the "substudy approach" are appropriate. To synthesize the evidence from the 25 studies, some metric has to be used. In a traditional survey where each study is discussed at length, the metric is often implicit and contained in mind of the reviewer. Splitting the studies into substudies is an attempt to make the metric explicit and to enable us to do a more systematic evaluation of the evidence.[16] For a more traditional survey of the literature, the reader is referred to Flanagan (1999).

Does Bargaining Coordination Matter for Economic Performance?

The indicators of bargaining coordination focus on multiple aspects of collective bargaining. It is, therefore, a reasonable starting point to ask what we learn from the 25 studies about the *combined* impact of centralization, concentration, informal coordination, and corporatism on different dimensions of economic performance. We summarize the findings of the 125 substudies in table 5-12 as a simple "vote count." Column one lists the relevant macroeconomic performance indicators. Column two lists the hypothesized relationship between the relevant performance indicator and bargaining coordination: positive (+), negative (-), U-shaped (U), Hump-shaped (H), and no relationship (N). The columns headed "rate 1," "rate 2," and "evaluation of evidence" summarize the empirical findings. "Rate 1" is the proportion of substudies that find evidence in support of the hypothesized relationship, and "rate 2" is the proportion of substudies that test for and find evidence of a hump- or U-shaped relationship.[17]

In the aggregate, about 60% of the substudies support the view that bargaining coordination affects economic outcomes in the predicted way.[18] However, as is evident from table 5-12, there is significant

---

15.   Each substudy is characterized in terms of the econometric methodology (estimation approach) and the type of data set (cross-country or pooled cross-country data set) used to estimate it; the time period considered; the type of test, if any, used to test the hump hypothesis; and the types of control variables used. Doing this makes it possible to analyze if the underlying attributes of the studies (such as the econometric methodology, data material, and time period) have any systematic influence on the pattern of results. The details are contained in appendix 2.

16.   The approach is similar in spirit to a meta-analysis of the underlying studies (see, for example, Bergh et al [1997: chapter 3]).

17.   If theory disagrees and predicts that the relationship can be either monotonic or nonmonotonic, then rate 1 refers to the total proportion of substudies that find evidence in favor of either type of relationship.

18.   Only two of the 125 substudies are a variance with the prediction of economic theory. The first of these is obtained by OECD (1997) and suggests that the employment rate is low in countries with high levels of bargaining coordination. The result is based on

Table 5-12. Bargaining Coordination and Economic Outcomes: A Summary and Evaluation of Results

Performance indicator [a]	Hypothesis [b]	Rate 1 [c]		Rate 2 [d]		Evaluation of evidence
		Percentage	n_1^e	Percentage	n_2^e	
The unemployment rate	−/H	70	40	44	16	Evidence of a negative relationship; little evidence of a hump-shaped relationship.
Inflation	−/H	30	20	9	11	Little evidence of any relationship.
The employment rate	+/U	42	12	36	11	Weak evidence of a U-shaped relationship.
Okun's index	−/H	75	12	100	2	Some evidence of a hump-shaped relationship but most of the evidence suggests that the relationship is negative.
Real compensation growth	−/H	56	9	20	5	Evidence of a negative relationship; almost no evidence of a hump-shaped relationship.
Productivity growth	+/U	38	8	50	6	Weak evidence of a U-shaped relationship.
Open economy index	−/H	50	8	100	2	Some evidence of a hump-shaped relationship, but most of the evidence suggests that the relationship is negative.
Wage dispersion	+	100	7	—	—	Strong evidence of a positive relationship.
Earnings inequality	+	80	5	20	5	Strong evidence of a positive relationship.
Index of job quality	+	100	2	—	—	Some evidence of a positive relationship.
Labor supply	+	100	1	—	—	Some evidence of a positive relationship.
Growth/inflation index	−	100	1	—	—	Some evidence of a negative relationship.

— Not available.

a. The performance indicators are either in levels (typically decade averages) or in first differences.

b. In column 2, for each of the 12 economic outcomes, we indicate what economic theory predicts about the relationship between the particular economic performance indicator and bargaining coordination.

c. Rate 1 = the proportion of substudies that find evidence of the expected relationship, and n_1 is the total number of substudies that investigates the relevant relationship.

d. Rate 2 = the proportion of substudies that test for and find evidence of a hump- or U-shaped relationship, and n_2 is the total number of substudies that perform a test for a hump- or U-shaped relationship.

e. n_1 is the total number of substudies that investigate the relevant relationship, and n_2 is the total number of substudies that perform a test of the hump hypothesis.

Note: All relationships are reported with reference to an increase in bargaining coordination. For example, a positive relationship means that the economic indicator increases as bargaining coordination increases, and a U-shaped relationship means that the economic indicator decrease at first and then starts rising at higher levels of coordination.

Source: Constructed from appendix 2.

variation in the level of confidence that we can place upon the relationship between individual macroeconomic performance indicators and bargaining coordination.[19] Countries with coordinated collective bargaining tend, *ceteris paribus*, to have lower unemployment rates than other countries. Studies that use composite measures of unemployment (such as Okun's index or the open economy index) confirm this tendency. The confidence in this finding is somewhat mitigated by the fact that very few (about one-third) of the relevant substudies find a positive relationship between the employment rate and bargaining coordination. The most robust result is that countries with a high level of bargaining coordination tend to have a more compressed wage distribution. This finding can be attributed to a number of causes, including egalitarian bargaining; the fact that centralized bargaining reduces the scope for firm- and/or industry-specific factors to enter wage contracts (Harcourt 1997); or to insurance motives (Agell and Lommerud 1992). Furthermore, Rowthorn (1992a, b) argues that wage dispersion is a proxy for job quality. He provides evidence that both the quantity of jobs (a high employment rate) and the quality of jobs (low wage dispersion) are higher in countries with coordinated collective bargaining.

In table 5-12, we attribute equal weight to all substudies irrespective of the kind of estimation approach used (whether simple correlation analysis or more sophisticated estimation approaches) and the kinds of data used (cross-country or pooled cross-country data sets). To judge the robustness of the results reported in tables 5-12 , we pool all substudies irrespective of macroeconomic indicators and divide them into three groups. In the first group, we include studies that used simple correlation analysis on cross-country data. In the second group, we include those studies that used the regression approach to analyze cross-country data. The third group contains those studies that apply regression techniques to analyze pooled cross-country data. Table 5-13 summarizes the results for each group as percentages of substudies that do and do not find evidence of a relationship between economic performance (in general) and bargaining coordination. The studies based on simple correlation analysis find significant relationships more often than those that

---

a simple correlation between the employment rate and OECD1997-3. The Spearman correlation is significant at the 10 percent level but only for 1994. For the years 1980 and 1990, the relationship is insignificant. Hence, the result is not very robust. The second result, obtained by Bean (1994), suggests that a high level of employee coordination (measured by LNJ1991-1) is associated with high unemployment. However, if the combined effect of employer and employee coordination is taken into account, the correlation is negative.

19.   In addition, if there is a tendency not to report insignificant results, then the reported numbers overstate the true significance of the relationship.

Table 5-13. Percentage of Substudies That Find a Relationship between Bargaining Coordination and Economic Outcomes, Disaggregated according to the Estimation Approach and Data Material Used

	Correlation approach	Regression approach with cross-country data	Regression approach with pooled cross-country data	Regression approach (total)
Relationship (percent)	73	53	67	57
No relationship (percent)	27	47	33	43
Number of substudies	53	50	22	72

Note: We construct the table by pooling the results for the 12 economic indicators and calculate the percentage of substudies that find a relationship (or no relationship) for each of the three groups. We construct the information in the last column from data on all substudies using the regression approach irrespective of the data used.

Source: Constructed from appendix 2.

use more advanced techniques. This suggests (unsurprisingly) that the more often and effectively one controls for cross-country differences in economic policy, in the institutional environment, and in economic conditions, the weaker the relationship between bargaining coordination and economic performance becomes. We conclude for this reason that there are good reasons to believe that the evidence in tables 5-12 exaggerates the importance of bargaining coordination.

Testing the Hump Hypothesis

The hump hypothesis has been explicitly tested in a number of studies (Calmfors and Driffill 1988; Dowrick 1993; Freeman 1988a; OECD 1988, 1997) accounting for 58 of the 125 substudies. The evidence in favor of the hump hypothesis is weak. Overall, only 21 of the substudies statistically "confirm" the hump hypothesis. The evidence for individual performance indicators is summarized in table 5-12 by "rate 2," and is at best mixed. The view that semicoordinated bargaining systems are associated with a relatively high unemployment rate is supported in fewer than half of the 16 substudies that address this question (rate 2 = 44 percent). The relationship between bargaining coordination and the employment rate is found in only one-third of the relevant 11 substudies (rate 2 = 36 percent) to be U-shaped. Half of the six substudies concerned with productivity growth find evidence of a U-shaped relationship between bargaining co-ordination and productivity growth.[20] The conclusion that the evidence in favor of the hump hypothesis is weak may, however, be sensitive to differences in the underlying estimation methodology and test procedure. To investigate this, we pool the 58 relevant substudies and divide them into three groups according to the type of test they employ to test the hump hypothesis. A similar decomposition is done with respect to estimation approach. The results are shown in table 5-14.

Three test procedures are used to test the hump hypothesis: the ranking test, the quadratic test, and the dummy variable test. In the ranking test, countries that have coordinated bargaining systems and those that

Table 5-14. Percentage of Substudies Testing the Hump Hypothesis That Find a Relationship between Bargaining Coordination and Economic Outcomes, Disaggregated according to Test Procedure and Estimation Approach Used

	Different test specification[a]			Different estimation approaches[b]	
	Dummy variable test	Quadratic test	Ranking test	Correlation	One-step regression
Hump/U-shaped relationship (percent)	11	40	41	35	38
No relationship (percent)	44	60	45	46	53
Monotonic relationship (percent)	44	0	14	19	9
Number of substudies	9	20	29	26	32

a. For each of the tests, the null hypothesis is that there is no hump/U-shaped relationship. The alternative hypothesis is that the relationship is hump/U-shaped.

b. We construct the frequency distribution by pooling the results for the eight relevant macroeconomic indicators and calculate the percentage of "hump/U-shaped relationships," "no relationships," and "monotonic relationships," respectively, for each of the groups of substudies.

Source: Constructed from appendix 2.

---

20.   Dowrick (1993) explains the U-shaped relationship between productivity growth and bargaining coordination as follows. Whether or not unions welcome or fight productivity-enhancing changes (new machinery or new working practices) depends on the elasticity of labor demand. If labor demand is inelastic, then unions are likely to fight productivity-enhancing changes because they would lead to layoffs. Hence, institutional changes that reduce the elasticity of labor demand, such as a move from firm-level to industry-level bargaining, mobilize unions to oppose technological progress and, ultimately, productivity growth may be relatively low in a semicentralized bargaining system.

have uncoordinated systems are ranked before those with semicoordinated bargaining systems (Calmfors and Driffill 1988: 22–23). This (new) ranking is then examined against the relevant macroeconomic performance indicator. A statistically significant relationship between the ranking and the relevant macroeconomic performance indicator is taken as evidence of the hump hypothesis. The ranking test has three drawbacks. First, the new ranking of countries can be somewhat arbitrary. Second, the test is effectively a test for a symmetric hump. Third, the ranking is often used as a cardinal variable, which it is not. In the quadratic test, the institutional indicator of interest and its square are included in a regression model. If the coefficient of the indicator itself is negative and that of its square is positive, then the relevant relationship is U-shaped. Conversely, if the coefficient of the indicator itself is positive and that of its square is negative, then the relevant relationship is hump-shaped. This test is more flexible than the ranking test in the sense that it does not assume symmetry and does not rely on an arbitrary reordering of countries. However, the problem that the relevant institutional indicator is included as a cardinal variable remains. The dummy variable test is performed by dividing the countries in the sample into three groups (coordinated, semicoordinated, and uncoordinated countries) and including a dummy variable for two of the groups in the relevant regression model. If the dummy variable for the group of countries with a semicoordinated bargaining system is significant, then the relationship is U- or hump-shaped (depending on the sign of the coefficient of the dummy variable). As with the ranking test, the main problem is the arbitrariness of the classification. The virtue of the test is that it avoids using bargaining coordination as a cardinal variable (OECD 1997). From table 5-14, we see that the main conclusion remains: irrespective of which test is used, the evidence in favor of the hump hypothesis is weak.[21] In addition, we see that the underlying estimation approach does not have any systematic influence on the results.

---

21.   The dummy variable test detects far fewer nonmonotonic relationships than the ranking and the quadratic tests, however. This supports the view that the "true relationship" is close to being monotonic (if not constant). The dummy variable test basically compares the average performance of the three groups of countries using the groups of countries with uncoordinated bargaining systems as the baseline. If the true relationship between, say, unemployment and bargaining coordination is only slightly hump-shaped, then the difference between the average performance of countries with uncoordinated and semicoordinated bargaining systems is rather small. Accordingly, the dummy variable test has a hard time detecting the true underlying "hump." The quadratic test and the ranking test, on the other hand, are more likely to detect the hump. Moreover, the evidence in table 5-15 suggests that the latter two may be equally effective in doing so.

Stability of the Relationship

An interesting pattern emerges when studies that focus on the 1970s and 1980s are compared with more recent studies that focus on the 1990s. Whereas the studies that analyze the 1970s and the 1980s (Calmfors and Driffill 1988, Cameron 1984, Tarantelli 1986) tend to support the view that bargaining coordination affects macroeconomic conditions, the support is much weaker for the 1990s (OECD 1997).[22] This suggests that the relationship between bargaining coordination and macroeconomic performance has been less pronounced in the 1990s. This is not entirely surprising. In fact, the observed differences between labor market systems in the 1970s and 1980s may simply reflect differences in their capacities to adapt to the supply shocks of the 1970s and the disinflationary policies of the 1980s. In the more stable environment of the 1990s, bargaining coordination has become less important relative to other determinants of macroeconomic performance. This suggests that the static benefits of bargaining coordination might not be that large, whereas the dynamic benefits are more clearly reflected in the evidence. This observation is supported by the fact that countries with widely different bargaining systems were performing equally well in the relatively stable environment of the 1960s. In recent times, the reduced importance of bargaining coordination as a determinant of economic performance is also related to changes in the economic environment. For example, globalization has exposed many industries to significant international competition, and changes in industry structure and the legislative framework in which collective bargaining takes place have increased the importance of nonunionized labor markets in many OECD countries (most notably in the United Kingdom and New Zealand). Both of these tendencies can help explain why bargaining coordination has become less important.[23]

Dissecting Bargaining Coordination

As discussed above, bargaining coordination refers to various formal and informal aspects of industrial relations systems such as employer and employee coordination, centralization, and union concentration. In

---

22. Dowrick (1993) can find only a (U-shaped) relationship between total factor productivity and bargaining coordination in the 1960s and 1970s. In the 1980s, he cannot identify any statistically significant relationship.

23. Empirically, Crouch (1990) and OECD (1997) find evidence that supports the view that exposure to international competition disciplines unions and reduces the performance differences among different bargaining systems.

previous sections, we did not attempt to distinguish between any of these aspects. In this section, we investigate how the different aspects of bargaining coordination have been found to relate to economic performance.

Formal and Informal Bargaining Coordination

Informal bargaining coordination is significant in countries like Germany, Japan, and perhaps Switzerland. We recall from table 5-6 that it matters a great deal for the measured degree of bargaining coordination in these countries whether informal bargaining coordination is taken into account or not. This raises the more general question: Do informal coordination mechanisms make a difference to the relationship between bargaining coordination and economic performance?

To answer this question, the substudies can be divided into those that focus exclusively on formal aspects of bargaining coordination (such as centralization and union concentration) and those that also take into account informal coordination.[24] Table 5-15 summarizes the results of these two groups of substudies. The evidence in table 5-15 suggests that the linkage between bargaining coordination and economic performance is more discernible when the focus is on formal coordination. When informal aspects of bargaining coordination are taken into account, fewer substudies (51 percent versus 70 percent) find a statistically significant

Table 5-15.   Percentage of All Substudies That Find a Relationship between Bargaining Coordination and Economic Outcomes, Disaggregated according to Formal and Informal Bargaining Coordination

	Formal bargaining coordination only	Formal and informal bargaining coordination
Relationship (percent)	70	51
No relationship (percent)	30	49
Number of substudies	84	41

Note: We construct the table by pooling the results from all 125 substudies and calculate the percentage of relationships (or no relationships) for each of the two groups.
Source: Constructed from appendix 2.

---

24.   The studies that take into account formal and informal coordination are the top seven ones listed in table 5-5. More specifically, the relevant indicators are D1993-2, LNJ1991-1, LNJ1991-2, LNJ1991-3, OECD1997-2, OECD1997-3, and S1990-1.

relationship between bargaining coordination and economic performance. This result is based on all 125 substudies. However, when we focus on only those substudies that test the hump hypothesis (see table 5-16), we find that those substudies that use an indicator of formal bargaining coordination rather than an indicator of formal and informal bargaining coordination support the hump hypothesis. When both formal and informal bargaining coordination are taken into account, either the relationship between bargaining coordination and economic performance becomes statistically insignificant or the statistical evidence points in the direction of a monotonic relationship.

These findings suggest that informal coordination can help remove the disadvantage associated with (formal) semicoordinated bargaining. However, since informal coordination by its very nature is not embodied in institutions or laws, instability is an important issue and informal coordination has a strong tendency to break down in times of rapid economic and social change. Although it is useful to think of informal coordination as a substitute for formal coordination, the two aspects of bargaining coordination are certainly not perfect substitutes.

Employer versus Employee Coordination

Bean (1994), Jackman (1993), and Scarpetta (1996) analyze the relative importance of employee and employer coordination in accounting for

Table 5-16. Percentage of Substudies Testing the Hump Hypothesis That Find a Relationship between Bargaining Coordination and Economic Outcomes Disaggregated according to Formal and Informal Bargaining Coordination

	Formal bargaining coordination only	Formal and informal bargaining coordination
Hump/U-shaped relationship (percent)	58	11
No relationship (percent)	39	63
Monotonic relationship (percent)	3	26
Number of substudies	31	27

Note: We construct the table by pooling the results from the 58 relevant substudies and calculate the percentage of "hump/U-shaped relationships," "no relationships," and "monotonic relationships" for each of the two groups of substudies.

Source: Constructed from appendix 2.

comparative unemployment performance.[25] Using different control variables and time periods, all three studies strongly indicate that employer coordination is more important than employee coordination. In other words, whereas more employer coordination always leads to lower unemployment, more employee coordination has a much smaller effect on unemployment (Jackman 1993), has no effect (Scarpetta 1996), or can even lead to higher unemployment (Bean 1994). Employer coordination can be more important than employee coordination because employers' organizations are more effective in controlling wage drift when bargaining takes place at different levels (from the plant to the national level) than unions. This can reduce wage competition among firms and the pressure for individual firms to give in to wage demands by unions. In addition, the cost of a labor conflict is reduced when employers bargain together rather than individually. This is because when they bargain together, they cannot steal business from each other during a strike.

Union Centralization versus Concentration

Union centralization amounts to the capacity of the national union confederation to influence wage levels and patterns across the economy, whereas union concentration is related to the number and type of unions at each level of bargaining (see table 5-4). Both are potentially important determinants of economic performance, but separating their respective effects is difficult as they are highly correlated; usually, high centralization is associated with high concentration.[26] However, Golden (1993) has made an attempt to do so. She finds that countries with a highly centralized *and* concentrated union structure tend to perform better (in terms of unemployment, inflation, Okun's index, and the open economy index) than others. The relative importance of the two is not clear, but Golden (1993) argues that concentration seems to be more important than centralization.

Bargaining Coordination and the Flexibility of the Labor Market

The evidence discussed above, suggests that cross-country differences in economic outcomes can be related to different levels of bargaining coordination. The studies reviewed in this section ask a different

---

25.   Employee coordination is measured by index LNJ1991-1 and employer coordination by LNJ1991-2. The correlation between the two is 0.65, which suggests that multicollinearity may be a problem.

26.   Cameron (1984) and Schmitter (1981) provide separate "centralization" and "concentration" rankings of 18 OECD countries (see S1981-2, S1981-3, C1984-2, and C1984-3). The correlation between the two sets of indicators is on the order of magnitude of 0.5–0.8.

question: how is bargaining coordination related to labor market flexibility? Labor market flexibility is a fuzzy concept but can be measured by indicators such as real wage flexibility, adjustment speed to wage shocks, unemployment persistence, and the job search effectiveness of unemployed workers (see table 5-9). Seven studies have used the two-step regression approach to estimate these indicators and have investigated the indicators' relationship with bargaining coordination. Table 5-17 summarizes the results of the studies

The two most interesting results relate to (real) wage flexibility and unemployment persistency (hysteresis).[27] First, hysteresis can arise because of membership effects (Blanchard and Summers 1986), because of loss of skills and discouraged-worker effects, and because of the depreciation of capital during a recession that does not fully recover subsequently or takes a long time doing so (Rowthorn 1995). Layard, Nickell, and Jackman (1991) find that *employer* coordination reduces persistence while *employee* coordination increases it. Subsequent research by Scarpetta (1996) suggests that the employer effect is, on average, greater and that unemployment in countries with semicoordinated bargaining systems shows a relatively high degree of persistence. In addition, Jackman, Pissarides, and Savouri (1990) provide evidence that the search effectiveness of unemployed workers is higher in countries with highly coordinated collective bargaining, suggesting that high bargaining coordination is associated with smaller discouraged-worker effects. Second, the evidence suggests that the (bargained) real wage is more responsive to employment conditions where bargaining coordination is high (Bean, Layard, and Nickell 1986; Layard, Nickell, and Jackman 1991). This combined with the faster adjustment to shock brings support to the notion that bargaining coordination helps the labor market absorb shocks fast and at low employment cost. This conclusion is further supported by a recent study by Blanchard and Wolfers (2000), who show that the interaction between shocks and institutions is crucial for explaining the cross-country and time-series variations in unemployment in the OECD over the last 40 years.

The Interaction between Bargaining Coordination, Union Density, and Coverage

The interaction between bargaining coordination, density, and coverage is important for our understanding of the relationship between

---

27.   We use the two terms, persistence and hysteresis, interchangeably. However, strictly speaking, hysteresis refers to a situation where the unemployment process has a unit root and therefore never returns to the original equilibrium after a shock. Persistence, on the other hand, refers to a situation where the unemployment process is *close* to having a unit root; therefore, it takes a long time for it to return to its original equilibrium.

Table 5-17. The Relationship between Indicators of Labor Market Flexibility and Bargaining Coordination: A Summary of the Relevant Studies

Study	Year	Performance indicator	Result
Layard, Nickell, and Jackman (1991)	1956–85	Real wage flexibility	Centralization/coordination (LNJ1991-1/2 and CD1998) increases real wage flexibility. Neocorporatism (T1986) has no effect on real wage flexibility.
McCallum (1986)	1974–83	Real wage flexibility	Centralization/coordination (MC1986) has no effect on real wage flexibility.
Newell and Symons (1987)	1955–83	Real wage flexibility	Centralization/coordination (NS1987) increases real wage flexibility. Evidence that semicoordinated systems have less real wage flexibility.
Bean, Layard, and Nickell (1986)	1956–85	Real wage flexibility	Centralization/coordination (BS1985) increases real wage flexibility.
Layard, Nickell, and Jackman (1991)	1956–85	Hysteresis	Employee coordination (LNJ1991-1) increases the persistence of unemployment, whereas employer coordination (LNJ1991-2) reduces it. Neocorporatism (T1986) has no effect on unemployment persistence.
Scarpetta (1996)	1970–93	Hysteresis	Aggregate employer and employee coordination (LNJ1991-1/2) reduces persistence. Both centralized and decentralized wage-setting (CD1998) systems are associated with low persistence, whereas semicentralized systems induce persistence.
Alogoskoufis and Manning (1988)	1951–86	Hysteresis	Find no evidence that persistence in unemployment is larger in Europe than in the United States and Japan.
Bean, Layard, and Nickell (1986)	1956–85	Adjustment speed to shocks	Corporatism (BS1985) increases adjustment speed to real wage shocks.
Newell and Symons (1987)	1955–83	Adjustment speed to shocks	Corporatist (NS1987) countries adjust faster to real wage shocks than noncorporatist countries.
Jackman, Pissarides, and Savouri (1990)	1971–88	Beveridge curve	The level of unemployment consistent with a given vacancy level is lower in centralized (CD1988) countries.

Source: Authors.

112

collective bargaining and economic performance. Table 5-18 shows the rank correlation between selected indicators of bargaining coordination, union density, and bargaining coverage, respectively. It appears that countries with a highly coordinated bargaining system tend to have high union density and high bargaining coverage.[28] Moreover, it is primarily the indicators that focus on centralization and formal employee and employer coordination that are positively correlated with union density and bargaining coverage. Those indicators that focus on informal coordination are, with one exception, not correlated with union density and bargaining coverage.[29] One interpretation of this

Table 5-18. Spearman Rank Correlation between Selected Indicators of Bargaining Coordination, Union Density, and Coverage of Collective Bargaining

Measure	Union density	Bargaining coverage
Bargaining centralization		
CD1988	0.71[a]	0.70[a]
OECD1997-1	0.44[a]	0.75[a]
C1984-1	0.88[a]	0.57[b]
S1981-1	0.65[b]	0.46[c]
Corporatism		
BS1985	0.34	0.46[c]
T1986	0.25	0.24
Employee or employer coordination		
LNJ1991-1	0.65[a]	0.56[b]
LNJ1991-2	0.43[b]	0.43[b]
Informal and formal coordination		
OECD1997-2	0.23	0.42[b]
S1990-1	0.32	0.17

Note: See table 5-5, for a more precise definition of the 10 indicators of bargaining coordination.
Significance levels:
a. 1 percent
b. 5 percent
c. 10 percent
Source: OECD (1997: tables 3.3 and 3.4) and own calculations.

---

28. While the correlation is positive, there are significant outliers. For instance, France has a relatively coordinated bargaining system, yet union density (but not coverage) is very low. Likewise, Japan combines a relatively coordinated bargaining system with low union density and coverage (see tables 5-2 and 5-6).
29. The same is true for the two indicators that focus on corporatism.

finding is that centralization of collective bargaining at the national level requires a broadly based union movement, in other words, high union density or at least high bargaining coverage. On the other hand, informal coordination between employers, as in Japan, can take place even if only a small proportion of the labor force is unionized and if collective agreements cover only a minority of workers.

Jackman (1993), Nickell (1997), and Nickell and Layard (1999) analyze the interaction among the three aspects of unionism and economic performance. The findings of Nickell (1997) are discussed in detail in box 5-1.

Box 5-1.   Regression to Explain Log Unemployment Rate Percentage

Nickell (1997) estimates the relationship between the logarithm to the unemployment rate and bargaining coordination, bargaining coverage, and union density in a pooled cross-section of 20 OECD countries in 1983–88 and 1989–94. He controls for unobserved country-specific random effects. The estimated equation for total unemployment is as follows:

$$u = 0.012UD + 0.45BCOV - 0.46BCOR + \beta X$$
$$\quad\quad (1.9) \quad\quad\quad (2.1) \quad\quad\quad (5.2)$$

where

u	=	The logarithm to the unemployment rate.
UD	=	Union density (unionized workers as a percentage of wage and salary earners).
$BCOV$	=	Bargaining coverage index (index 1 is low, index 2 is medium, and index 3 is high bargaining coverage).
$BCOR$	=	Employer and employee coordination index (ranging from 2 to 6 with index 2 as the lowest and index 6 as the highest level of bargaining coordination).
X	=	Control variables, including employment protection, replacement rate, benefit duration, active labor market policies, total tax rate, and change in inflation.

The numbers in the parentheses are t-statistics.

An increase in bargaining coverage by one index point increases (the natural) logarithm to unemployment by 0.45, so unemployment increases by about 56 percent. Starting from a baseline unemployment rate of 5 percent this means that the unemployment rate would, other things being equal, increases to 8 percent. However, if bargaining coordination at the same time increases with one index point the adverse effect is nullified. Hence, Nickell (1997: 72) concludes that high levels of unionization and union coverage do not appear to have serious implications for average levels of unemployment so long as they are offset by high levels of coordination in wage bargaining, particularly among employers.

They confirm the findings that bargaining coverage and, to a lesser extent, union density have a negative effect on unemployment at a given level of bargaining coordination and that bargaining coordination has a positive impact on unemployment for given bargaining coverage. However, if bargaining coverage and bargaining coordination increase together (as the correlation coefficients in table 5-18 suggest), the adverse impact on unemployment disappears, especially if employers drive coordination. Thus, the apparently negative relationship between coverage and performance can be countered by coordination of collective bargaining. Moreover, Layard, Nickell, and Jackman (1991: 137) argue that it is the failure of studies such as Calmfors and Driffill (1988) to take into account the impact of bargaining coverage on economic performance that gives the (misleading) impression that semicoordinated collective bargaining is "bad."[30] Overall, these results underscore the danger of focusing on individual aspects of labor market institutions when the interaction between many different aspects determines outcomes. Labor market institutions complement each other, and a comparison between different "packages of institutions" may be the most sensible way to assess their macroeconomic performance.

Strikes, Social Partnership, and International Trade

The previous sections examined the evidence on the relationship between bargaining coordination and economic outcomes. Although illuminating in many respects, the discussion would not be complete without looking at some additional economic and social aspects of collective bargaining and economic performance. To this end, we review some additional findings that relate to strikes, social partnership, and international trade.

Strikes

Strikes can be viewed as an intermediate indicator that links economic performance to underlying institutional structures (such as union density, bargaining coverage, and bargaining coordination). In most countries,

---

30.   In this argument, it is implicitly assumed that the econometric studies fail to control for bargaining coverage when they estimate the impact of bargaining coordination on economic performance. While this is true for many studies (for example, Calmfors and Driffill 1988), it is not true for OECD (1997). However, a comparison between the results obtained from a simple correlation analysis (OECD 1997: table 3.5, p. 75) and the results obtained from a regression model that controls for bargaining coverage and union density (OECD 1997: table 3.6, p. 76) weakly supports the interpretation of Layard, Nickell, and Jackman (1991).

the percentage of working time lost because of strikes is trivial, less than one-tenth of 1 percent (Booth 1995: table 2.2; Polachek and Siebert 1993: table 10.3).[31] This suggests that the parties in the labor market usually reach an agreement and that it is the strike *threat* rather that an actual strike that affects the outcome of collective bargaining (Siebert and Addison 1981). Nevertheless, it is important to notice that the frequency and nature of strikes can depend on how collective bargaining is organized and that these differences can have an impact on economic performance.

The evidence on the impact of bargaining coordination on strikes is clear: Bargaining coordination reduces strike activity.[32] This suggests that a coordinated bargaining system can produce social peace because it either helps to institutionalize a distributional norm or improves the flow of information and thereby reduces the risk that a strike would occur because of the workers' misconception about the firm's profitability. The link between strike activity and economic performance is also fairly clear. Cameron (1984) has investigated the relationship between the number of working days lost to strikes during the period 1965–81 in 18 industrial countries and various measures of economic performance. He finds that countries with a high level of strike activity are associated with high inflation, high unemployment rates, and fast-growing average earnings.

Social Partnership

The successful implementation of income policies during the 1960s and 1970s based on triparty negotiations in Scandinavia and elsewhere in the OECD are probably the best known examples of social partnerships. Since then social dialogue has continued to play a role in some European countries, but has not been a success everywhere and has disappeared in countries where it used to play a role. More recently the International Labour Organisation has documented how tripartite agreements among employers, unions, and governments have, by and large, been unsuccessful in countries like the Czech Republic, Hungary, and the Russian Federation (ILO 1997). In other parts of the world such as in Latin America, tripartism has, however, helped to ensure the implementation of stabilization programs (ILO 1997). Likewise, Israeli unions played an important role in

---

31.   Although this a low figure on aggregate (for example, less than a working day per worker per year—this is much lower than absenteeism), it can still have macroeconomic implications, for example, if it is concentrated in key sectors such as transport and banking services.

32.   Strike activity is typically measured as the number of days lost because of strikes per 1,000 workers in the labor force per year or the log of the number of workers involved in conflict per 1,000 workers; see Cameron (1984), Crouch (1985, 1990), and Hibbs (1978).

designing a politically acceptable stabilization program in the mid-1980s (Pencavel 1995). In other cases, stabilization programs have failed because they did not gain sufficient backing from the population (see, for example, the discussion of Venezuela at the beginning of the 1990s and of Zambia in 1985 in Freeman 1993b: 139).

Systematic evidence about the impact of social partnerships on economic performance is scanty although some political scientists have made attempts to quantify the effects. In a sequence of papers, Lange and Garrett[33] have looked at the interaction between the strength of labor, party control, and economic outcomes. They argued that labor market parties, particularly unions, expect the government to deliver certain welfare goods and policies in exchange for wage moderation and peace in the labor market. They identify four scenarios, which are summarized in table 5-19.

In scenario (1), unions are powerful, in the sense that the majority of workers are unionized, bargaining is controlled by national organizations, and the government is left-wing. Under these circumstances, economic performance is predicted to be "good." This is because the pursuit of welfare policies by left-wing parties is likely to lead to voluntary wage moderation. Moreover, as pointed out by Olson (1982), if unions organize the majority of workers, they are less likely to engage in wasteful rent-seeking because unionized workers are going to bear most of the costs associated with these activities themselves. In scenario (2), unions are politically weak, in the sense that union density is low and bargaining is decentralized, and the government is right-wing. Under these circumstances, "good" economic performance can also be expected. This is because unions are restricted in their wage demands by competitive pressure from product markets that are left unregulated by the right-wing government. In scenarios (3) and (4), "bad" economic performance

Table 5-19.   The Hypothesis of Coherence

Union characteristic	Left-wing government	Right-wing government
Powerful	(1) Good economic performance	(3) Bad economic performance
Weak	(4) Bad economic performance	(2) Good economic performance

Source: Authors.

---

33.   Alvarez, Garrett, and Lange (1991); Garrett and Lange (1986), and Lange and Garrett (1985).

is to be expected. This is because there is a mismatch between the power of the labor movement and the political orientation of the government. If, for instance, a right-wing government coexists with powerful unions, the unions are unlikely to restrict their wage demands voluntarily because the government cannot be expected to deliver any welfare goods in return. Likewise, a left-wing government coexisting with weak unions cannot count on any voluntary wage moderation because individual unions are likely to pursue their own interests (wage pressure) without taking into account the economy-wide consequences of their actions.

To test "the hypothesis of coherence," the political orientation of the government and the organizational power of unions are interacted in a multiple regression. [34] Using economic growth as the key economic indicator, the hypothesis finds some support in a sample of OECD countries (Alvarez, Garrett, and Lange 1991, Garrett and Lange 1986; Lange and Garrett 1985).[35]

International Trade and Wage Discipline and Compression

To the extent that international trade increases competition in product markets (and nonunionized labor markets), union behavior can be affected. Theoretical reasoning suggests that competitive product markets can be an important determinant of wage restraint (Layard, Nickell, and Jackman 1991 and others). If firms are exposed to competition, they cannot pass wage demands on to consumers as higher prices and stay in business. Therefore, both sides of the labor market bear the consequences of high wage settlements.

What does the empirical evidence suggest about the relationship between bargaining coordination and international trade? By means of statistical evidence from 13 industrial countries from the period 1960 to 1985, Crouch (1990) finds that strike activity, inflation, and the unemployment rate tend to be relatively low in countries where unions are concentrated in sectors exposed to international competition.[36] This may be taken as evidence that exposure to international trade and the associated competitive pressure significantly disciplines unions. Crouch (1990: 70)

---

34.   The index that measures the "organizational power of labor" is described in appendix 1 (see also table 5-5, where it has the code name GL1985). The political orientation of the government is measured by the "index of left-wing party control of government." Again, a description can be found in appendix 1.

35.   As pointed out by Beck and Katz (1995), some of these findings are due to artifacts of the econometric technique being used. However, the results for growth in GDP are robust to more appropriate econometrics techniques. The findings for other performance indicators such as unemployment and inflation are not.

36.   See appendix 1 for more information about how union concentration in sectors exposed to international competition is measured.

puts it in the following way: "Those in the exposed sector are likely to be more concerned with problems of international competitiveness than those in the protected sector... and less able to treat the consequences of their actions as something that can be absorbed within a general national development." OECD (1997) shows that exposure to foreign competition[37] significantly reduces the difference, in terms of the unemployment rate and inflation, between countries with semicoordinated and countries with highly coordinated bargaining systems. In other words, countries with semicoordinated collective bargaining (at the industry or sector level) perform as well as countries with fully coordinated collective bargaining, provided that import penetration is high (high import ratio). They also perform better than countries with uncoordinated bargaining systems. Overall, it seems that exposure to foreign competition can help to remove the disadvantage (if any) associated with semicoordinated wage bargaining. More generally, the studies by Crouch (1990) and OECD (1997) show that it is dangerous to try to assess the impact of collective bargaining on economic performance without paying attention to differences in the economic environment.

An interesting but often overlooked, feature of collective bargaining is its capacity to provide insurance against shocks arising from international markets. This comes about because collective bargaining leads to a compression of the wage distribution, as documented above. The logic of the theoretical argument is this. A risk-averse worker who is uncertain about his or her future wage would have an incentive to buy insurance against the wage risk. Although this kind of insurance is not privately provided, different types of labor market institutions that reduce the uncertainty of future labor earnings, such as collective bargaining, minimum wages, and unemployment insurance, can serve as substitutes (Agell and Lommerud 1992). An important source of uncertainty about future wages is a country's openness to international trade and the process of globalization. Agell (1998) investigates empirically the relationship between indicators of exposure to external risk[38] and labor market institutions, such as centralization of collective bargaining, minimum wages (relative to average wages), and unemployment benefits (the replacement ratio). In support of the insurance argument, he finds that countries that are more exposed to external risks tend to have a more compressed wage structure, more centralized systems of collective bargaining, a higher replacement ratio, and a higher relative minimum wage.

---

37. Measured by the import ratio, which is imports as a percentage of GDP. The same results can be obtained using exports as a percentage of GDP.
38. A measure of the volume of trade.

Conclusion

The evidence on the macroeconomic impact of collective bargaining in OECD countries is too weak and fragile to warrant generalizations. It appears though that the interaction cannot be analyzed in isolation from the general economic and political environment in which bargaining takes place, as industrial relations develop endogenously in response to country-specific economic, legal, and political conditions. It is therefore dangerous to extrapolate results derived from average cross-country performance to specific countries. Nevertheless, a number of more specific results do emerge. These are broadly in line with the findings of Flanagan (1999) in his recent survey of the literature. The results are as follows:

- The hump hypothesis receives little support, except for selected indicators such as unemployment and productivity, and in these cases the evidence is not very robust. The view that countries with coordinated bargaining systems, on average, performed better than countries with less coordinated system in the 1970s and 1980s receives some support, but the differences seem to have disappeared in the 1990s. This suggests that the static benefits of bargaining coordination might not be that great, whereas the dynamic benefits seem to be larger, that is, bargaining coordination facilitates faster and more flexible responses to shocks.
- The most robust result relates to wage dispersion and earnings inequality. Countries with coordinated collective bargaining tend to have less wage dispersion than other countries.
- Cross-country variation in union density has little impact on economic performance. High bargaining coverage, on the other hand, tends to be associated with relatively poor economic performance.
- In countries with high bargaining coverage, the adverse impact on unemployment can be counteracted if bargaining takes place in a coordinated fashion. This suggests that one aspect of collective bargaining cannot be analyzed in isolation from other aspects. In other words, it seems to be the interaction between various aspects of collective bargaining that determines the macroeconomic impact: complementarity between different institutions is crucial.
- In countries that lack formal bargaining coordination (in the form of centralized bargaining between national organizations), informal bargaining coordination can arise as a substitute. The instability of informal coordination makes it less than a perfect substitute, though.

Appendix 1

Definition and Description of the Indicators of Bargaining Coordination

Code: BK1996.
Focus: Centralization.
Reference period: 1970s and 1980s.
Reference: Blau and Kahn 1996.
Definition: The index is a simple average of CD1988, S1981-1, C1984-1, and an index taken from Blyth (1979).
Type: Subjective.
Scale: Ranking (in descending order of centralization).
Country ranking: Hungary, Austria, the United States, Switzerland, the United Kingdom, Germany, Norway (in 1982 and 1989), Italy, Sweden, and Australia.
Comments: It is unclear what is gained by averaging the indicators. It is a problem that the four indicators do not refer to the same period. Hungary is classified as the country with the most coordinated bargaining system because of state control.

Code: C1990-1.
Focus: Labor movement centralization.
Reference period: 1960s, 1970s, and 1980s.
Reference: Crouch 1990.
Definition: The index is derived from Visser's index of vertical integration (level of centralization) of the main confederation (Visser 1990). It is based on the following variables (a) the level of control over strike decisions, (b) the allocation of finance and staff resources, (c) characteristic bargaining levels, (d) the role of officials in bargaining, and (e) an index of the power of exposed-sector unions (see C1990-2).
Type: Subjective.
Scale: The index is constructed using an additive score. Low numbers refer to a low degree of "labor movement centralization."

Country ranking: The numbers in parentheses refer to the score for the 1960s, 1970s, and 1980s, respectively (Dowrick 1993: table 3.2). Austria (10.5,10.5,10.5), Belgium (6,6,6), Denmark (5,4.5,4.5), Finland (5.0,7.5,7.5), France (1,1,1), Germany (6.5,6.5,6.5), Ireland (2.5,3,3), Italy (2,3.5,3.5), Netherlands (9.5,7.5,7), Norway (9.5,9,8), Spain (n.a.,n.a., 1), Sweden (8.5,8,8), Switzerland (3,3,3), and the United Kingdom (2,2,2).
Comments: The indicator focuses on the employee side, disregarding the employer side of industrial relations.

Code: C1990-2.
Focus: Power of exposed-sector unions.
Reference period: 1960s, 1970s, and 1980s.
Reference: Crouch 1990.
Definition: The index is the proportion of all unionized workers who are members of one of the five largest "industry-type" unions in the exposed sectors of the economy. The exposed sectors of the economy are defined as those that are subject to international competition.
Type: Subjective.
Scale: Cardinal scale.
Country ranking: The numbers in parentheses refer to the score for the 1960s, 1970s, and 1980s, respectively (see Dowrick 1993: table 3.2). Austria (35.3,33.14,29.32), Belgium (23.61,22.16,20.67), Denmark (16.1,14.36,12.16), Finland (18.04,24.18,21.42), France (17.48,10.93,21.44), Germany (45.52,46.71,44.52), Ireland (7.21,7.56,5.55), Italy (11.22,10.54,14.22), Netherlands (24.45,21.85,23.36), Norway (28.22,26.47,20.16), Spain (n.a.,n.a.,19.7), Sweden (24.10,27.95,19.13), Switzerland (25.10,23.45,21.04), and the United Kingdom (17.71,16.72,12.33).

Code: D1993-1 and D1993-2.
Focus: Centralization and coordination of collective bargaining, respectively.
Reference period: The two indexes are constructed for three decades: the 1960s, the 1970s, and the 1980s.
Reference: Dowrick 1993.
Definition: The index of union centralization is derived from Crouch (1990) (C1990-1) and Calmfors and Driffill (1988) (CD1998) and is defined as the level of centralization of the main union confederation. The index of coordination is an adjustment of the former index, taking into account the information on informal coordination in Soskice (1990) (S1990-1) (only the scores for Japan and Switzerland are adjusted).
Type: Subjective.
Scale: 2 (decentralized/uncoordinated) to 6 (centralized/coordinated).

Country ranking: The numbers in parentheses refer to each of the three time periods. **D1993-1 (centralization)**: Australia (4,4,5), Austria (6,6,6), Belgium (4,4,4), Canada (2,2,2), Denmark (5.3,4.8,4.8), Finland (3.2,4.8,4.8), France (3.3,3.3,3.3), Germany (4.5,4.5,4.5), Ireland (2.8,4.5,3.3), Italy (1.9,3.3,3.3), Japan (3,3,3), Netherlands (5.4,4.3,4), New Zealand (4,4,4), Norway (5.3,5.0,4.4), Sweden (5.3,5,5), Switzerland (3,3,3), the United Kingdom (3.3,3.3,2), and the United States (2,2,2). **D1993-2 (coordination)**: Australia (4,4,5), Austria (6,6,6), Belgium (4,4,4), Canada (2,2,2), Denmark (5.3,4.8,4.8), Finland (3.2,4.8,4.8), France (3.3,3.3,3.3), Germany (4.5,4.5,4.5), Ireland (2.8,4.5,3.3), Italy (1.9,3.3,3.3), Japan (6,6,6), Netherlands (5.4,4.3,4), New Zealand (4,4,4), Norway (5.3,5.0,4.4), Sweden (5.3,5,5), Switzerland (5,5,5), the United Kingdom (3.3,3.3,2), and the United States (2,2,2).

Code: GL1985.
Focus: Organizational power of labor.
Reference period: 1965–80.
Reference: Garrett and Lange 1986 and Lange and Garrett 1985.
Definition: The index of organizational power of labor is derived from Cameron (1984) (C1984-1). It is the sum of the standardized (a) union density, (b) power of confederations in collective bargaining, (c) scope of collective bargaining, and (d) degree of organizational unity.
Type: Subjective/objective.
Scale: See below under C1984-1.
Country ranking: In order of decreasing power of organized labor: Sweden, Norway, Austria, Denmark, Finland, Belgium, the United Kingdom, Netherlands, Ireland, Australia, West Germany, Italy, Canada, the United States, France, and Japan.
Comments: GL1985 differs from C1984-1 because it includes the scope of bargaining (union density). This makes a difference for the ranking and scores of countries.

Code: MC1986.
Focus: Corporatism.
Reference period: 1970s.
Reference: McCallum 1986.
Definition: The index is derived from Crouch (1985) and therefore is based on information on (a) centralization of the union movement, (b) the degree of shop floor autonomy, (c) coordination among employers, and (d) the presence of work councils.
Type: Subjective/objective.
Scale: Scale from 0 (low level of corporatism) to 4 (high level of corporatism).

Country ranking: Australia (0), Canada (0), France (0), Ireland (0), the United Kingdom (0), the United States (0), Belgium (0.5), Italy (0.5), New Zealand (0.5), Finland (1.5), Japan (1.5), Switzerland (2), Denmark (3), Austria (4), Germany (4), Netherlands (4), Norway (4), and Sweden (4).
Comments: Notice that the indicator takes employer coordination into account.

Code: NS1987.
Focus: Corporatism.
Reference period: 1955–83.
Reference: Newell and Symons 1987.
Definition: Heuristic definition: "Corporatism is a set of institutions where the interests of organizations of labor and capital are brought together in a framework with the state in which a high level of employment is sought by limitations of wage demands." The classification of countries is based on a detailed description of the five countries included in the study. It is stressed that a necessary condition for corporatism is that lower-level bargaining units adhere to what is decided at higher levels (absence of wage drift).
Type: Subjective.
Scale: Classification of countries.
Countries: The United States: noncorporatist; Germany: corporatist until 1977, thereafter noncorporatist; the United Kingdom: corporatist until 1979, thereafter noncorporatist; Japan: noncorporatist until 1975, thereafter corporatist; Sweden: corporatist.

Code: OECD1997-1, OECD1997-2, and OECD1997-3.
Focus: Bargaining centralization, bargaining coordination, bargaining centralization and coordination, respectively.
Reference period: Indicators constructed for three points in time: 1980, 1990, 1994.
Reference: OECD 1997.
Definition: Two separate indexes are constructed. The first is defined according to the prevailing level of collective bargaining and makes up the index of bargaining centralization (OECD1997-1). The second index is defined according to the degree of coordination (formal and informal) among and between employers and employees (OECD1997-2). The two indexes are combined into one index (or classification of countries in three groups) of centralization and coordination (OECD1997-3).
Type: Objective/subjective.
Scale: Countries are assigned to a scale from 1 to 3. Centralized/coordinated is 3 and decentralized/uncoordinated is 1. From this, a ranking is constructed, and the countries are divided into three groups.

Country ranking: Combined centralization and coordination grouping.
In 1980: *High:* Sweden, Finland, Austria, Australia, Denmark, Norway,
and Germany; *Medium:* Spain, Belgium, Japan, Netherlands, and Swit-
zerland; *Low:* France, Canada, Italy, New Zealand, Portugal, the United
Kingdom, and the United States. **In 1990:** *High:* Sweden, Finland, Aus-
tria, Australia, Norway, and Germany; *Medium:* Denmark, France, Spain,
Belgium, Japan, Netherlands, Switzerland, and Portugal; *Low:* Canada,
Italy, New Zealand, the United Kingdom, and the United States. **In 1994:**
High: Italy, Finland, Austria, Norway, and Germany; *Medium:* Sweden,
Denmark, France, Spain, Belgium, Japan, Netherlands, Switzerland, and
Portugal; *Low:* Canada, New Zealand, the United Kingdom, the United
States, and Australia.

Code: LNJ1991-1 and LNJ1991-2.
Focus: Employee and employer coordination, respectively.
Reference period: 1980s.
Reference: Layard, Nickell, and Jackman 1991.
Definition: Two indexes (one for employers and one for employees) are
constructed on the basis of country-specific information on (a) the cen-
tralization of collective bargaining and (b) informal coordination among
firms and unions.
Type: Subjective.
Scale: Countries are divided into three groups. 1 = Low level of coordi-
nation, 2 = intermediate level, and 3 = high level of coordination. The
combined index (LNJ1991-1/2) is derived as the sum of the scores of
LNJ1991-1 and LNJ1991-2.
Country ranking: Employer coordination (LNJ1991-2): *High:* Denmark,
Germany, Austria, Finland, Norway, Sweden, and Switzerland; *Medium:*
Belgium, France, Portugal, Spain, and Japan; *Low:* Ireland, Italy, the
United States, the United Kingdom, New Zealand, and Australia. **Em-
ployee coordination (LNJ1991-1):** *High:* Denmark, Sweden, Norway,
Finland, and Austria; *Medium:* Belgium, France, Germany, Italy, Nether-
lands, Portugal, Spain, Australia, New Zealand, and Japan; *Low:* Swit-
zerland, the United States, Canada, and Ireland.

Code: S1981-1, S1981-2, and S1981-3.
Focus: Corporatism, union centralization, and union concentration, re-
spectively.
Reference period: 1960s and 1970s.
Reference: Schmitter 1981.
Definition: S1981-1 consists of two subindexes: an index of union cen-
tralization (S1981-2) and an index of union concentration (S1981-3). Cen-
tralization is measured as (a) the confederation's role in collective

bargaining, (b) the confederation's control over strikes, (c) the size of the confederation's staff relative to membership, and (d) the proportion of the membership dues accruing to the confederation. Union concentration is measured as (a) the number of national confederations, (b) whether manual and nonmanual employees are organized in different unions, and (c) whether national unions and confederations include stable factions.
Type: Objective/subjective.
Scale: S1981-1 is constructed by adding the ranking of countries according to their ranking on the centralization and union monopoly dimension.
Country ranking: S1981-1 (declining degree of corporatism): Austria, Norway, Denmark, Finland, Sweden, Netherlands, Belgium, West Germany, Switzerland, Canada, Ireland, the United States, France, the United Kingdom, and Italy.
Comments: The subindexes (S1981-2 and S1981-3) can be used separately (Golden 1993). The main problem is that the behavior of the employer side is underdeveloped.

Code: C1984-1, C1984-2, and C1984-3.
Focus: Organizational power of labor, union centralization, and union concentration, respectively.
Reference period: 1965–80.
Reference: Cameron 1984.
Definition: The index of organizational power of labor (C1984-1) is made up of three components: union centralization, union concentration, and union density. Union centralization is measured by the extent to which confederations (a) consult with unions about wage negotiations prior to collective bargaining, (b) themselves participate in collective bargaining, (c) possess the right to veto negotiated settlements, and (d) control the distribution of strike funds to unions. This defines C1984-2. Union concentration is measured by the number of confederations and unions affiliated with them. This defines C1984-3. Union density is measured as the average proportion of the work force being unionized during the period 1965 to 1980.
Type: Subjective but based on some objective observations.
Scale: The three subindexes are combined into the index of organizational power of labor (C1984-1) by adding the index of union centralization (C1984-2) and concentration (C1984-3) and multiplying by the density rate.
Country ranking: C1984-1 (declining power of organized labor): Sweden, Norway, Austria, Belgium, Finland, Denmark, Netherlands, Germany, the United Kingdom, Australia, Ireland, Switzerland, Italy, Canada, the United States, Japan, France, and Spain.

Comments: Besides the two subindexes, C1984-2 and C1984-3, Cameron (1984) constructs an index of the level at which wage bargaining takes place and an index of the presence of work councils and codetermination. However, none of these enters the overall index (S1984-1). The main problem is that the behavior of the employer side is not explicitly considered. The index of organizational power of labor (C1984-1) is almost identical to S1981-1.

Code: S1990-1.
Focus: Economy-wide coordination.
Reference period: The mid- to late-1980s.
Reference: Soskice 1990.
Definition: Both formal and informal coordination between workers and employers are taken into account. A bargaining system is said to be coordinated if it is either highly centralized or informally coordinated. Coordination among workers as well as among employers is taken into account. The overall score is the maximum of the coordination score for either workers or employers, not a weighted average.
Type: Subjective measurement.
Scale: Countries are ranked on a scale from 0 to 5, with 0 being the lowest degree of coordination and 5 the highest.
Country ranking: The United States (0), the United Kingdom (0), France (1.5), Italy (2), Netherlands (3), Germany (3.5), Sweden (4), Norway (4), Switzerland (4), Austria (5), and Japan (5).
Comments: Soskice includes only countries that he knows well in this sample.

Code: S1990-2.
Focus: Wage drift.
Reference period: The late 1980s.
Reference: Soskice 1990.
Definition: This index is a judgment of how much wage pressure would arise in the absence of external pressure from employers' organizations and national unions. The index takes into account the capacity to produce wage drift (strong local unions) and the incentive to do so (long-term relationships versus short-term maximization).
Type: Subjective measurement.
Scale: Countries are ranked on a two-dimensional scale ranging from 1 to 4, with 1 being the lowest level of "local pushfulness" and 4 the highest.
Country ranking: The United States (1), Japan (1), Switzerland (1), Netherlands (2), Germany (2), Sweden (2), Norway (2), Austria (2), Italy (2.5), France (3), and the United Kingdom (4).

Comments: The measure is subjective; moreover, it tries to answer a hypothetical question.

Code: CD1988.
Focus: Centralization.
Reference period: The mid-1980s.
Reference: Calmfors and Driffill 1988.
Definition: This index measures the formal extent of interunion and interemployer cooperation in wage bargaining with the other side. Information on (a) the formal level of wage-setting/coordination within central (employers' and employees') organizations and (b) the existence of parallel central organizations and their cooperation is used to construct CD1988.
Type: Subjective.
Scale: Countries are ranked according to the formal level of wage-setting (firm, industry, or national) and the existence of parallel national organizations and their cooperation. The overall score is the sum of the two subscores, with 6 being the highest level of centralization and 0 the lowest. Two alternative rankings are provided to perform a ranking test of the hump hypothesis. The first alternative ranking (A) is constructed by taking first the most centralized country, then the most decentralized country, then the second-most centralized country, and so on. The second alternative ranking (B) is constructed by taking first the three most centralized countries followed by the three most decentralized countries, and so on.
Country ranking: (in declining order of centralization) Austria (6), Norway (5), Sweden (5), Denmark (5-), Finland (5-), Germany (5-), Netherlands (4+), Belgium (4), New Zealand (4), Australia (4), France (3+), the United Kingdom (3+), Italy (3+), Japan (3), Switzerland (3), the United States (2), and Canada (2).

Code: T1986.
Focus: Neocorporatism.
Reference period: 1968–83.
Reference: Tarantelli 1986.
Definition: The index is constructed by allocating a number (1 = very low to 5 = very high) to each of the following three dimensions (a) the degree of neocorporatism of trade unions (the degree of political and ideological consensus between the labor market parties and the government and the extent to which trade unions and employers' organizations are integrated into the political process); (b) the centralization of collective bargaining (the level at which bargaining takes place, the organizational centralization of trade unions, the degree of centralization of collective bargaining in the main employers' organization, and the

existence and working of trilateral institutions that assist collective bargaining); and (c) the degree of neoregulation of industrial conflict (the actual process of settling labor disputes).
Type: Subjective measure.
Scale: The scores are added up to give an overall score from 1 to 15 (the high number is a high level of neocorporatism).
Country ranking: (in declining order of neocorporatism) Austria (15), Germany (14), Japan (13), Sweden (12), Denmark (12), Norway (12), Australia (10), Netherlands (10), Finland (10), Belgium (9), the United States (9), Canada (9), New Zealand (8), France (7), the United Kingdom (5), and Italy (4).

Code: BS1985.
Focus: Corporatism.
Reference period: 1970s.
Reference: Bruno and Sachs 1985.
Definition: The index is derived from Crouch 1985. It has four additive components (a) union centralization, (b) shop-floor autonomy, (c) employers' coordination, and (d) the presence of work councils.
Type: Subjective indicator.
Scale: A low level of corporatism is zero and a high level is 4, cardinal scale.
Country ranking: (in descending order of corporatism) Austria, West Germany, Netherlands, Sweden, Norway, Switzerland, Denmark, Finland, Belgium, Japan, New Zealand, the United Kingdom, France, Italy, Australia, Canada, and the United States.

Code: C1985.
Focus: Neocorporatism.
Reference period: 1970s.
Reference: Crouch 1985.
Definition: Neocorporatism is defined as an industrial relations system in which "an entirely coordinated union movement has developed within a political context responsive to labor demands. In liberal industrial relations systems, the labor movement lacks any significant centralized coordination, irrespective of labor's political place in society."
Type: Subjective.
Scale: Two classes: neocorporatist and liberal.
Countries: Neocorporatist: Austria, Denmark, Norway, Sweden, Netherlands, Switzerland, Finland, and West Germany. **Liberal:** Australia, Belgium, Canada, France, Ireland, Italy, Japan, New Zealand, the United Kingdom, and the United States.
Comments: The main problem is that employer coordination is not included in the analysis.

Code: B1996.
Focus: Corporatism and centralization.
Reference period: The 1980s.
Reference: Bleaney 1996.
Purpose: To capture elements of both centralization and corporatism.
Definition: This is a combination of BS1985 and CD1988.
Type: Subjective.
Scale: 1 = highly centralized, 2 = decentralized, 3 = moderately centralized but highly corporatist, 4 = moderately centralized and no corporatism.
Country ranking: 1 = Austria, Norway, and Sweden; 2 = Switzerland, Canada, Japan, and the United States, 3 = West Germany, Denmark, Finland, and the Netherlands; 4 = France, Italy, the United Kingdom, Australia, Belgium, and New Zealand.
Comments: BS1985 refers to the 1970s and includes an element of centralization, whereas CD1988 refers to the 1980s. It is hence a problem to merge the two indicators.

Code: H1987.
Focus: Corporatism.
Reference period: The 1970s.
Reference: Heitger 1987.
Definition: BS1985 is recoded. Countries that have either high levels of corporatism or low levels of corporatism are ranked above those with intermediate levels of corporatism.
Type: Subjective.
Scale: Cardinal scale from 1 to 9.
Countries: Austria (1), the United States (1), Canada (2), West Germany (2), Australia (3), Netherlands (3), Italy (4), Norway (4.5), Sweden (4.5), France (5), Switzerland (6), the United Kingdom (6), Denmark (7), New Zealand (7), Finland (8), Japan (8), and Belgium (9).

Code: C1984-5
Focus: Index of left-wing party control of government.
Reference period: 1965–82.
Reference: Cameron 1984.
Definition: The index combines two properties (a) the extent to which left-wing parties control government as indicated by their share of portfolio positions in the cabinet; and (b) the strength of the governing left-wing party in the parliament.
Type: Objective.

Scale: For each country, the proportion of cabinet seats held by left-wing parties in each month of each year is calculated and multiplied by the share of the seats in parliament held by left-wing governments. The average over 18 years (1965–82) is then taken.

Country ranking: (in descending order of "leftism") Austria, Sweden, the United Kingdom, Germany, Norway, Denmark, Finland, Australia, Belgium, Switzerland, Netherlands, France, Italy, Ireland, Spain, Japan, Canada, and the United States.

Appendix 2

Substudies

Overview

The statistical evidence contained in the 25 studies (see footnote 13 in chapter 5) that have investigated the relationship between indicators of bargaining coordination and macroeconomic performance has been decomposed into 125 substudies. A substudy (that is, the unit of analysis) is defined as a relationship between a specific indicator of bargaining coordination (defined in table 5-5) vis-à-vis a specific economic indicator (defined in table 5-7 or table 5-8). All the substudies are listed in appendix 3. For each substudy, the table provides the following information: (a) the source of the study; (b) the period to which it refers; (c) whether the institutional indicator focuses on formal ("formal") or on formal and informal ("informal") aspects of the bargaining system; (d) the code for the institutional indicator; (e) a description of the economic indicator; (f) a characterization of the relationship between the institutional indicator and the performance indicator; (g) if the hump hypothesis is tested, we indicate which test were used (ranking, quadratic or dummy variable test); (h) the estimation approach (correlation or regression approach); (i) the number of observations in the relevant data set; (j) the type of the data set (cross-country or pooled cross-country data); (k) whether attempts were made to control for other aspects of the institutional environment; (l) whether economic or political control variables were used; (m) econometric technique used; (n) whether sensitivity analysis were carried out. Table A-1 provides a summary of the evidence contained in table A-2.

Table A-1. The Relationship between Bargaining Coordination and Economic Outcomes: Aggregate Evidence from 125 Substudies

Economic outcome	Hypothesis	+	−	U	H	N	Substudies that tested the hump hypothesis	All substudies
Unemployment rate	−/H	1	21	0	7	11	16	40
Inflation	−/H	0	5	0	1	14	11	20
Employment rate	+/U	1	1	4	0	6	11	12
Okun's index	−/H	0	7	0	2	3	2	12
Real compensation growth	−/H	0	4	0	1	4	5	9
Open economy index	+/U	0	2	3	2	4	2	8
Productivity growth	−/H	0	0	0	0	5	6	8
Wage dispersion	+	0	7	0	0	0	0	7
Earnings inequality	+	0	4	1	0	0	5	5
Index of job quality	+	2	0	0	0	0	0	2
Labor supply	+	1	0	0	0	0	0	1
Growth/inflation index	−	0	1	0	0	0	0	1
Sum		5	52	8	13	47	58	125

Note: (1) All relationships are reported with reference to an increase in bargaining coordination. For example, a positive relationship means that the economic indicator increases as bargaining coordination increases, and a U-shaped relationship means that the economic indicator decreases at first and then starts rising at higher levels of coordination. (2) Column 8 refers to the number of substudies that explicitly investigate the hump hypothesis.

Source: Constructed from table A-2.

(table continues on following page)

Table A-2.   The Relationship between Bargaining Coordination and Economic Outcomes: Results from 125 Substudies

Study	Reference period	Formal/ informal bargaining coordination	Institutional indicator	Economic indicator	Result	Type of hump test	Estimation approach	Number of observations	Type of data set	Institutional control variables	Economic or policy control variables	Analysis method	Sensitivity analysis
Calmfors and Driffill (1988)	1974–85	Formal	C1964-1	Employment rate	U-shaped	Ranking test	Correlation	17	Cross	No	No	Correlation	No
Calmfors and Driffill (1988)	1974–85	Formal	CD1988	Employment rate	U-shaped	Ranking test	Correlation	17	Cross	No	No	Correlation	No
Freeman (1988a)	1979–85	Formal	C1985	Employment rate	PMR		Regression	12 or 19	Cross	Yes	Yes	OLS	Yes
Rowthorn (1992b)	1973	Formal	CD1988	Employment rate	NR	Quadratic test	Regression	17	Cross	No	No	OLS	No
Rowthorn (1992b)	1985	Formal	CD1988	Employment rate	U-shaped	Quadratic test	Regression	17	Cross	No	No	OLS	No
Rowthorn (1992a)	1973	Formal	CD1988	Employment rate	NR	Quadratic test	Regression	17	Cross	No	No	OLS	No
Rowthorn (1992a)	1985	Formal	CD1988	Employment rate	U-shaped	Quadratic test	Regression	17	Cross	No	No	OLS	No
OECD (1997)	1980–94	Informal	OECD1997-3	Employment rate	NR	Dummy variable test	Regression	57	Pooled	Yes	No	Correlation	No
OECD (1997)	1994	Informal	OECD1997-4	Employment rate	NMR	Ranking test	Correlation	19	Cross	No	No	Correlation	No
OECD (1997)	1990	Informal	OECD1997-4	Employment rate	NR	Ranking test	Correlation	19	Cross	No	No	Correlation	No
OECD (1997)	1980	Informal	OECD1997-4	Employment rate	NR	Ranking test	Correlation	19	Cross	No	No	Correlation	Yes
OECD (1997)	1980–94	Informal	OECD1997-4	Employment rate	NR	Quadratic test	Regression	57	Pooled	Yes	No	OLS	Yes
Bleaney (1996)	1973–82	Formal	B1996	Inflation	H-shaped	Ranking test	Regression	17	Cross	Yes	Yes	OLS	Yes
Bleaney (1996)	1983–89	Formal	B1996	Inflation	NR	Ranking test	Regression	17	Cross	Yes	Yes	OLS	Yes
Bleaney (1996)	1973–82	Formal	BS1985	Inflation	NR		Regression	17	Cross	Yes	Yes	OLS	Yes

135

Table A-2 continued

Study	Reference period	Formal/informal bargaining coordination	Institutional indicator	Economic indicator	Result	Type of hump test	Estimation approach	Number of observations	Type of data set	Institutional control variables	Economic or policy control variables	Analysis method	Sensitivity analysis
Bleaney (1996)	1983–89	Formal	BS1985	Inflation	NR		Regression	17	Cross	Yes	Yes	OLS	No
Golden (1993)	1974–85	Formal	C1984-2 (concent.)	Inflation	NMR		Regression	14	Cross	Yes	No	OLS/ boot-strap	No
Golden (1993)	1974–85	Formal	C1984-3 (central.)	Inflation	NR		Regression	14	Cross	Yes	No	OLS/ boot-strap	Yes
Crouch (1985)	1965–80	Formal	C1985	Inflation	NMR		Correlation	18	Cross	No	Yes	Graphical	Yes
Crouch (1990)	1960s, 1970s, and 1980s	Formal	C1990-1	Inflation	NMR		Correlation	13	Cross	No	No	Correlation	No
Crouch (1990)	1960s, 1970s, and 1980s	Formal	C1990-2	Inflation	NMR		Correlation	13	Cross	No	No	Correlation	No
OECD (1988)	1971–80	Formal	CD1988	Inflation	NR	Dummy/ graphic	Correlation	17	Cross	No	No	Graphic	No
OECD (1988)	1981–86	Formal	CD1988	Inflation	NR	Dummy/ graphic	Correlation	17	Cross	No	No	Graphic	No
Bleaney (1996)	1973–82	Formal	CD1988	Inflation	NR	Quadratic test	Regression	17	Cross	Yes	Yes	OLS	No
Bleaney (1996)	1983–89	Formal	CD1988	Inflation	NR	Quadratic test	Regression	17	Cross	Yes	Yes	OLS	No
OECD (1997)	1980–94	Informal	OECD1997-3	Inflation	NMR	Dummy variable test	Regression	57	Pooled	Yes	No	OLS	No
OECD (1997)	1980	Informal	OECD1997-4	Inflation	NR	Ranking test	Correlation	19	Cross	No	No	Correlation	Yes
OECD (1997)	1990	Informal	OECD1997-4	Inflation	NR	Ranking test	Correlation	19	Cross	No	No	Correlation	No
OECD (1997)	1994	Informal	OECD1997-4	Inflation	NR	Ranking test	Correlation	19	Cross	No	No	Correlation	No
OECD (1997)	1980–94	Informal	OECD1997-4	Inflation	NR	Quadratic test	Regression	57	Pooled	Yes	No	OLS	Yes
Golden (1993)	1974–85	Formal	S1981-2 (concent.)	Inflation	NR		Regression	14	Cross	Yes	No	OLS/ boot-strap	No
Golden (1993)	1974–85	Formal	S1981-3 (cent.)	Inflation	NR		Regression	14	Cross	Yes	No	OLS/ boot-strap	No

(table continues on following page)

136

Table A-2 continued

Study	Reference period	Formal/informal bargaining coordination	Institutional indicator	Economic indicator	Result	Type of hump test	Estimation approach	Number of observations	Type of data set	Institutional control variables	Economic or policy control variables	Analysis method	Sensitivity analysis
Nickell and Layard (1999)	1989–94	Informal	LNJ1991-1/2	Labor supply	PMR		Regression	20	Cross	Yes	Yes	GLS	No
Soskice (1990)	1985–89	Informal	S1990C-1	Unemployment	NMR		Regression	11	Cross	Yes	No	OLS	Yes
Soskice (1990)	1985–89	Formal	S1990-2	Unemployment	NMR		Regression	11	Cross	Yes	No	OLS	No
Bleaney (1996)	1973–82	Formal	B1996	Unemployment	H-shaped	Ranking test	Regression	17	Cross	Yes	Yes	OLS	Yes
Bleaney (1996)	1983–89	Formal	B1996	Unemployment	H-shaped	Ranking test	Regression	17	Cross	Yes	Yes	OLS	Yes
Bleaney (1996)	1973–82	Formal	BS1985	Unemployment	NMR		Regression	17	Cross	Yes	Yes	OLS	No
Bleaney (1996)	1983–89	Formal	BS1985	Unemployment	NMR		Regression	17	Cross	Yes	Yes	OLS	No
Calmfors and Driffill (1988)	1974–85	Formal	C1984-1	Unemployment	H-shaped	Ranking test	Correlation	17	Cross	No	Yes	Correlation	Yes
Cameron (1984)	1965–80	Formal	C1984-1	Unemployment	NMR		Correlation	18	Cross	No	No	Correlations	No
Cameron (1984)	1965–80	Formal	C1984-2	Unemployment	NMR		Correlation	18	Cross	No	No	Correlations	No
Golden (1993)	1974–85	Formal	C1984-2 (ccncent.)	Unemployment	NE		Regression	14	Cross	Yes	No	OLS/boot-strap	No
Cameron (1984)	1965–80	Formal	C1984-3	Unemployment	NMR		Correlation	18	Cross	No	No	Correlations	Yes
Golden (1993)	1974–85	Formal	C1984-3 (central.)	Unemployment	NR		Regression	14	Cross	Yes	No	OLS/boot-strap	Yes
Freeman (1988a)	1979–85	Formal	C1985	Unemployment	NMR		Regression	12 or 19	Cross	Yes	Yes	OLS	No
Crouch (1990)	1960s, 1970s, and 1980s	Formal	C1990-1	Unemployment	NMR		Correlation	13	Cross	No	No	Correlation	No
Crouch (1990)	1960s, 1970s, and 1980s	Formal	C1990-2	Unemployment	NMR		Correlation	13	Cross	No	No	Correlation	No
OECD (1988)	1981–86	Formal	CD1988	Unemployment	H-shape	Dummy variable test	Correlation	17	Cross	No	No	Graphic	No
Calmfors and Driffill (1988)	1974–85	Formal	CD1988	Unemployment	H-shaped	Ranking test	Correlation	17	Cross	No	Yes	Correlation	No

(table continues on following page)

Table A-2 continued

Study	Reference period	Formal/informal bargaining coordination	Institutional indicator	Economic indicator	Result	Type of hump test	Estimation approach	Number of observations	Type of data set	Institutional control variables	Economic or policy control variables	Analysis method	Sensitivity analysis
Rowthorn (1992a)	1985	Formal	CD1988	Unemployment	H-shaped	Quadratic test	Regression	17	Cross	No	Yes	OLS	No
Scarpetta (1996)	1983–93	Formal	CD1988	Unemployment	H-shaped	Quadratic test	Regression	181	Pooled	Yes	Yes	GLS	No
OECD (1988)	1971–80	Formal	CD1988	Unemployment	NMR	Dummy/graphic	Correlation	17	Cross	No	No	Graphic	No
Bleaney (1996)	1973–82	Formal	CD1988	Unemployment	NR	Quadratic test	Regression	17	Cross	Yes	Yes	OLS	No
Bleaney (1996)	1983–89	Formal	CD1988	Unemployment	NR	Quadratic test	Regression	17	Cross	Yes	Yes	OLS	No
Rowthorn (1992a)	1973	Formal	CD1988	Unemployment	NR	Quadratic test	Regression	17	Cross	No	Yes	OLS	No
Jackman (1993)	1983–88	Informal	LNJ1991-1	Unemployment	NMR		Regression	20	Cross	Yes	Yes	OLS	Yes
Scarpetta (1996)	1983–93	Informal	LNJ1991-1	Unemployment	NR		Regression	181	Pooled	Yes	Yes	GLS	Yes
Bean (1994)	1956–92	Informal	LNJ1991-1	Unemployment	PMR		regression	720	Pooled	Yes	Yes	WLS	No
Nickell and Layard (1999)	1989–94	Informal	LNJ1991-1/2	Unemployment	NMR		Regression	20	Cross	Yes	Yes	GLS	No
Bean (1994)	1956–92	Informal	LNJ1991-2	Unemployment	NMR		Regression	720	Pooled	Yes	Yes	WLS	No
Jackman (1993)	1983–88	Informal	LNJ1991-2	Unemployment	NMR		Regression	20	Cross	Yes	Yes	OLS	No
Jackman (1993)	1983–88	Informal	LNJ1991-1	Unemployment	NMR		Regression	20	Cross	Yes	Yes	OLS	Yes
Scarpetta (1996)	1983–93	Informal	LNJ1991-2	Unemployment	NMR		Regression	181	Pooled	Yes	Yes	GLS	Yes
OECD (1997)	1980–94	Informal	OECD1997-3	Unemployment	NMR	Dummy variable test	Regression	57	Pooled	Yes	No	CLS	No
OECD (1997)	1980	Informal	OECD1997-4	Unemployment	NR	Ranking test	Correlation	19	Cross	No	No	Correlation	Yes
OECD (1997)	1990	Informal	OECD1997-4	Unemployment	NR	Ranking test	Correlation	19	Cross	No	No	Correlation	Yes
OECD (1997)	1994	Informal	OECD1997-4	Unemployment	NR	Ranking test	Correlation	19	Cross	No	No	Correlation	No
OECD (1997)	1980–94	Informal	OECD1997-4	Unemployment	NR	Quadratic test	Regression	57	Pooled	Yes	No	OLS	Yes
Golden (1993)	1974–85	Formal	S1981-2 (concent.)	Unemployment	NMR		Regression	14	Cross	Yes	No	OLS/boot-strap	No

(table continues on following page)

Table A-2 continued

Study	Reference period	Formal/ informal bargaining coordination	Institutional indicator	Economic indicator	Result	Type of hump test	Estimation approach	Number of observations	Type of data set	Institutional control variables	Economic or policy control variables	Analysis method	Sensitivity analysis
Golden (1993)	1974–85	Formal	S1981-3 (cent.)	Unemployment	NR		Regression	14	Cross	Yes	No	OLS/ boot-strap	Yes
Nickell and Layard (1999)	1989–94	Informal	LNJ1991-1/2	Unemployment, long term	NMR		Regression	20	Cross	Yes	Yes	GLS	No
Nickell and Layard (1999)	1989–94	Informal	LNJ1991-1/2	Unemployment, short term	NMR		Regression	20	Cross	Yes	Yes	GLS	No
Cameron (1984)	1965–80	Formal	C1984-2	Compensation (growth)	NMR		Correlation	18	Cross	No	No	Correlation	No
Cameron (1984)	1965–80	Formal	C1984-3	Compensation (growth)	NMR		Correlation	18	Cross	No	No	Correlation	No
Freeman (1988a)	1979–85	Formal	C1985	Compensation (growth)	NMR		Regression	12 or 19	Cross	Yes	Yes	OLS	Yes
Cameron (1984)	1965–80	Formal	C1984-1	Compensation (growth)	NMR		Correlation	18	Cross	No	No	Correlation	No
OECD (1997)	1980–94	Informal	OECD1997-3	Compensation (growth)	NR	Dummy variable test	Regression	57	Pooled	Yes	No	OLS	Yes
OECD (1997)	1980–94	Informal	OECD1997-4	Compensation (growth)	H-shaped	Quadratic test	Regression	57	Pooled	Yes	No	OLS	Yes
OECD (1997)	1980	Informal	OECD1997-4	Compensation (growth)	NR	Ranking test	Correlation	19	Cross	No	No	Correlation	No
OECD (1997)	1990	Informal	OECD1997-4	Compensation (growth)	NR	Ranking test	Correlation	19	Cross	No	No	Correlation	Yes
OECD (1997)	1994	Informal	OECD1997-4	Compensation (growth)	NR	Ranking test	Correlation	19	Cross	No	No	Correlation	Yes
OECD (1997)	1980–94	Informal	OECD1997-3	Earnings inequality	NMR	Dummy variable test	Regression	57	Pooled	Yes	No	OLS	Yes
OECD (1997)	1980	Informal	OECD1997-4	Earnings inequality	NMR	Ranking test	Correlation	19	Cross	No	No	Correlation	No

(table continues on following page)

Table A-2 continued

Study	Reference period	Formal/informal bargaining coordination	Institutional indicator	Economic indicator	Result	Type of hump test	Estimation approach	Number of observations	Type of data set	Institutional control variables	Economic or policy control variables	Analysis method	Sensitivity analysis
OECD (1997)	1990	Informal	OECD1997-4	Earnings inequality	NMR	Ranking test	Correlation	19	Cross	No	No	Correlation	No
OECD (1997)	1994	Informal	OECD1997-4	Earnings inequality	NMR	Ranking test	Correlation	19	Cross	No	No	Correlation	No
OECD (1997)	1980–94	Informal	OECD1997-4	Earnings inequality	U-shaped	Quadratic test	Regression	57	Pooled	Yes	No	OLS	Yes
Blau and Kahn (1996)	1980–90	Formal	BK1996	Wage dispersion	NMR		Regression	10	Cross	No	Yes	OLS	Yes
Freeman (1988a)	1979–85	Formal	C1985	Wage dispersion	NMR		Correlation	12 or 19	Cross	No	No	Correlation	Yes
Freeman (1988a)	1979–85	Formal	CD1988	Wage dispersion	NMR		Correlation	12 or 19	Cross	No	No	Correlation	No
Rowthorn (1992b)	1973	Formal	CD1988	Wage dispersion	NMR		Correlation	17	Cross	No	No	Graphical	No
Rowthorn (1992b)	1985	Formal	CD1988	Wage dispersion	NMR		Correlation	17	Cross	No	No	Graphical	No
Rowthorn (1992a)	1973	Formal	CD1988	Wage dispersion	NMR		Correlation	17	Cross	No	No	Correlation	No
Rowthorn (1992a)	1985	Formal	CD1988	Wage dispersion	NMR		Correlation	17	Cross	No	No	Correlation	No
Bruno and Sachs (1985)	1965–80	Formal	BS1985	Growth/inflation index	NMR		Correlation	17	Cross	No	Yes	OLS	Yes
Rowthorn (1992b)	1973	Formal	CD1988	Index of job quality	PMR		Correlation	17	Cross	No	No	Graphical	No
Rowthorn (1992b)	1985	Formal	CD1988	Index of job quality	PMR		Correlation	17	Cross	No	No	Graphical	No
Calmfors and Drifill (1988)	1974–85	Formal	C1984-1	Okun's index	H-shaped	Ranking test	Correlation	17	Cross	No	Yes	Correlation	Yes

(table continues on following page)

Table A-2 continued

Study	Reference period	Formal/informal bargaining coordination	Institutional indicator	Economic indicator	Result	Type of hump test	Estimation approach	Number of observations	Type of data set	Institutional control variables	Economic or policy control variables	Analysis method	Sensitivity analysis
Golden (1993)	1974–85	Formal	C1984-2 (concent.)	Okun's index	NMR		Regression	14	Cross	Yes	No	OLS/boot-strap	No
Golden (1993)	1974–85	Formal	C1984-3 (central.)	Okun's index	NR		Regression	14	Cross	Yes	No	OLS/boot-strap	Yes
Crouch (1985)	1965–80	Formal	C1985	Okun's index	NMR		Correlation	18	Cross	No	Yes	Graphical	Yes
Crouch (1990)	1960s, 1970s, and 1980s	Formal	C1990-1	Okun's index	NMR		Correlation	13	Cross	No	No	Correlation	No
Crouch (1990)	1960s, 1970s, and 1980s	Formal	C1990-2	Okun's index	NMR		Correlation	13	Cross	No	No	Correlation	No
Calmfors and Drifill (1988)	1974–85	Formal	CD1988	Okun's index	H-shaped	Ranking test	Correlation	17	Cross	No	Yes	Correlation	No
McCallum (1986)	1974–83	Formal	MC1986	Okun's index	NMR		Regression	18	Cross	Yes	Yes	OLS	Yes
McCallum (1986)	1983–84	Formal	MC1986	Okun's index	NMR		Regression	18	Cross	Yes	Yes	OLS	Yes
Golden (1993)	1974–85	Formal	S1981-2 (concent.)	Okun's index	NR		Regression	14	Cross	Yes	No	OLS/boot-strap	Yes
Golden (1993)	1974–85	Formal	S1981-3 (cent.)	Okun's index	NR		Correlation	14	Cross	Yes	No	OLS/boot-strap	No
Tarantelli (1986)	1968–83	Formal	T1986	Okun's index	NMR		Correlation	16	Cross	No	No	Correlations	Yes
Calmfors and Drifill (1988)	1974–85	Formal	C1984-1	Open economy index	H-shaped	Ranking test	Correlation	17	Cross	No	Yes	Correlation	No
Golden (1993)	1974–85	Formal	C1984-2 (concent.)	Open economy index	NR		Regression	14	Cross	Yes	No	OLS/boot-strap	No
Golden (1993)	1974–85	Formal	C1984-3 (central.)	Open economy index	NR		Regression	14	Cross	Yes	No	OLS/boot-strap	Yes
Calmfors and Drifill (1988)	1974–85	Formal	CD1988	Open economy index	H-shaped	Ranking test	Correlation	17	Cross	No	Yes	Correlation	No
Golden (1993)	1974–85	Formal	S1981-2 (concent.)	Open economy index	NR		Regression	14	Cross	Yes	No	OLS/boot-strap	Yes

(table continues on following page)

Table A-2 continued

Study	Reference period	Formal/informal bargaining coordination	Institutional indicator	Economic indicator	Result	Type of hump test	Estimation approach	Number of observations	Type of data set	Institutional control variables	Economic or policy control variables	Analysis method	Sensitivity analysis
Golden (1993)	1974–85	Formal	S1981-3 (cent.)	Open economy index	NR		Regression	14	Cross	Yes	No	OLS/boot-strap	No
Soskice (1990)	1985–89	Informal	S1990-1	Open economy index	NMR		Regression	11	Cross	Yes	No	OLS	Yes
Soskice (1990)	1985–89	Formal	S1990-2	Open economy index	NMR		Regression	11	Cross	Yes	No	OLS	Yes
Heitger (1987)	1960s	Formal	BS1985	Growth (GNP/cap)	NR	Ranking test	Regression	34	Pooled	No	Yes	OLS	Yes
Heitger (1987)	1970s	Formal	BS1985	Growth (GNP/cap)	U-shaped	Ranking test	Regression	34	Pooled	No	Yes	OLS	No
Nickell and Layard (1999)	1989–94	Informal	LNJ1991-1/2	Growth in labor productivity	NR		Regression	20	Cross	Yes	Yes	GLS	No
Dowrick (1993)	1980–89	Formal	D1993-1	Growth, TFP	NR	Quadratic test	Regression	18	Cross	No	Yes	OLS	Yes
Dowrick (1993)	1960–90	Formal	D1993-1	Growth, TFP	U-shaped	Quadratic test	Regression	54	Cross	No	Yes	OLS	Yes
Dowrick (1993)	1980–89	Informal	D1993-2	Growth, TFP	NR	Quadratic test	Regression	18	Cross	No	Yes	OLS	Yes
Dowrick (1993)	1960–90	Informal	D1993-2	Growth, TFP	U-shaped	Quadratic test	Regression	54	Cross	No	Yes	OLS	No
Nickell and Layard (1999)	1989–94	Informal	LNJ1991-1/2	Growth, TFP	NR		Correlation	20	Cross	Yes	Yes	GLS	No

Note: A substudy is defined as a relationship between a specific indicator of bargaining coordination vis-à-vis a specific economic outcome. The following categories are used:

PMR Positive monotonic relationship between the institutional indicator and the relevant economic performance indicator.

NMR Negative monotonic relationship between the institutional indicator and the relevant economic performance indicator.

NR No statistically significant relationship between the institutional indicator and the relevant economic performance indicator.

H-shaped A hump-shaped relationship between the institutional indicator and the relevant economic performance indicator is identified.

U-shaped A U-shaped relationship between the institutional indicator and the relevant economic performance indicator is identified.

All relationships are reported with reference to an increase in bargaining coordination. Each substudy is characterized in terms of the estimation approach (correlation or regression approach) and the type of data set (cross-country or pooled cross-country data set) used, the time period considered, the type of test, if any, used to test the hump hypothesis, the type of control variables used, econometric technique used (OLS, WLS etc.), whether the empirical specification was based on a theoretical model, and whether sensitivity analysis was carried out.

Source: Constructed by the authors.

Selected Glossary

bargaining coordination. Bargaining coordination refers to the extent of coordination between unions and employers' organizations in wage bargaining. Six different aspects of bargaining coordination can be identified: union centralization, union concentration, employer centralization, level of collective bargaining, informal coordination, and corporatism.

bargaining coverage. Bargaining coverage is the number of workers, unionized or not, whose pay and employment conditions are determined by a collective agreement as a percentage of all workers, both unionized and nonunionized.

corporatism. Corporatism is a combination of (a) high union density and bargaining coverage and a high degree of union and employer centralization/concentration and (b) social partnership between national workers' and employers' organizations and the government.

economic rent. A payment to a factor of production in excess of what is necessary to keep it at its present supply.

employer centralization. The capacity of the national employers' confederation to influence wage levels and patterns across the economy is known as employer centralization.

hump-shaped relationship. The relationship between two variables, x and y, is hump-shaped if y is increasing in x for low values of x and decreasing for high values of x.

individual performance pay/merit pay. This is a wage system in which the wage rate is directly related to the performance of the individual employee.

informal coordination. Informal coordination of collective bargaining between unions and employers' organizations/firms can take many forms. Two common mechanisms of informal coordination are (a) informal consultations at the industry, regional, or national level between unions and firms and (b) pattern bargaining.

level of bargaining. Collective bargaining typically takes place at three different levels: the firm level, the industry level, and the regional/national level.

multilevel bargaining system. A bargaining system in which collective bargaining takes place at many levels (including the firm, the industry, and the regional/national levels) at the same time is referred to as a multilevel bargaining system.

pattern bargaining. The collective agreement in a dominant section is mimicked by other sectors.

reservation wage. The wage level below which the worker will not supply his or her labor; the wage that makes the worker indifferent to the choice of whether to work or not to work.

super-normal profits. Profits in excess of competitive (normal) profits; that is, revenue which exceeds all opportunity costs of the firms.

Tobins q. The market value of the firm relative to the replacement cost of the firm's assets.

union centralization. Union centralization is the capacity of the national union confederation to influence wage levels and patterns across the economy.

union concentration. Union concentration refers to the number of unions that represent workers at different levels of collective bargaining. Union concentration is high if "few" unions at the relevant level of bargaining are representing workers.

union density. The number of workers who are members of a union as a percentage of all workers is known as union density.

U-shaped relationship. The relationship between two variables, x and y, is U-shaped if y is decreasing in x for low values of x and increasing for high values of x.

wage drift. Wage drift refers to the local increase in the wage rate in addition to that specified in the collective agreement reached at the regional or national level.

wage pressure. Wage pressure refers to the wage demands of workers, unions, and firms (efficiency wages).

References

Acs, Z. J., and D. B. Audretsch. 1987. "Innovation in Large and Small Firms." *Economics Letters* 23: 109–12.

Addison, J. T., and B. T. Hirsch. 1989. "Union Effects on Productivity, Profits, and Growth: Has the Long Run Arrived?" *Journal of Labor Economics* 7(1): 72–105.

Agarwala, R. 1983. "Price Distortions and Growth in Developing Countries." Staff Working Paper no. 575. World Bank, Washington, D.C.

Agell, J. 1998. "Social Norms, Labor Market Institutions, and Economic Performance." Working Paper. Uppsala University, Department of Economics. Uppsala, Sweden.

Agell, J., and K. E. Lommerud. 1992. "Union Egalitarianism as Income Insurance." *Economica* 59: 295–310.

Aidt, T. 1997. "Cooperative Lobbying and Trade Policy." *Public Choice* 93: 455–75.

Allen, S. G. 1984. "Trade Unions, Absenteeism, and Exit-Voice." *Industrial and Labor Relations Review* 37(3): 331–45.

_____. 1988. "Unions and Job Security in the Public Sector." In R. Freeman and C. Ichniowski, eds., *When Public Sector Workers Unionize*, Chicago: University of Chicago Press.

Alogoskoufis, G. S., and A. Manning. 1988. "Wage-Setting and Unemployment Persistence in Europe, Japan, and the USA." *European Economic Review* 32: 698–706.

_____. 1991. "Tests of Alternative Wage Employment Bargaining Models with an Application to the UK Aggregate Labor Market." *European Economic Review* 35(1): 23–37.

Alvarez, R. M., G. Garrett, and P. Lange. 1991. "Government Partisanship, Labor Organization, and Macroeconomic Performance." *American Political Science Review* 85(2): 539–56.

Arudsothy, P., and C. R. Littler. 1993. "State Regulation and Union Fragmentation in Malaysia." In S. Frenkel, ed., *Organized Labor in the Asia-Pacific Region: A Comparative Study of Trade Unionism in Nine Countries*. Cornell International Industrial and Labor Relations Report no. 24. New York: ILR Press.

Bean, C. R. 1994. "European Unemployment: A Retrospect." *European Economic Review* 38: 523–34.

Bean, C. R., and P. J. Turnbull. 1988. "Employment in the British Coal Industry: A Test of the Labour Demand Model." *Economic Journal* 98: 1092–1104.

Bean, C. R., P. R. G. Layard, and S. J. Nickell. 1986. "The Rise in Unemployment: A Multi-country Study." *Economica* 53: S1–S22.

Bean, C. R., and J. Symons. 1989. "Ten Years of Mrs. T." In O. J. Blanchard and S. Fischer, eds., *NBER Macroeconomics Annual 4*. Cambridge, Mass. and London: MIT Press.

Beck, N., and J.N. Katz. 1995. "What to Do (and What Not to Do) With Time Series Cross-Section Data." *American Political Science Review* 89: 634–47.

Bellman, D. 1992. "Unions, the Quality of Labor Relations, and Firm Performance." In L. Mishel and P. B. Voos, eds., *Unions and Economic Competitiveness*. New York: M. E. Sharpe.

Bergh, J. C. J. M. van den, K. J. Button, P. Nijkamp, and G. C. Pepping. 1997. *Meta-Analysis in Environmental Economics*. Dordrecht: Kluwer Academic Publishers.

Betcherman, G. 1991. "The Effect of Unions on the Innovative Behaviour of Firms in Canada." *Industrial Relations Journal* 22(2): 142–51.

Bhattacherjee, D. 1987. "Union-Type Effects on Bargaining Outcomes in Indian Manufacturing." *British Journal of Industrial Relations* 22(2): 247–66.

Blanchard. O., and L. Summers. 1986. "Hysteresis and the European Unemployment Problem." In S. Fischer, ed., *NBER Macroeconomics Annual 1*. Cambridge, Mass. and London: MIT Press.

Blanchard, O., and J. Wolfers. 2000. "The Role of Shocks and Institutions in the Rise of European Unemployment: The Aggregate Evidence." *Economic Journal* 110: C1–33.

Blanchflower, D. G. 1996a. "Product Market Competition, Wages, and Productivity: International Evidence from Establishment-Level Data." *Annals d'Economie et de Statistique* 41/42 (June): 219–54.

_____. 1996b. "The Role and Influence of Trade Unions in the OECD." London School of Economics , Centre for Economic Performance Discussion Paper, no. 310. London, United Kingdom.

_____. 1997. "Changes over Time in Union Relative Wage Effects in Great Britain and the United States." Technical Report Working Paper no. 6100. , National Bureau of Economic Research, Cambridge, Mass.

Blanchflower, D. G., and S. Burgess. 1996. "New Technology and Jobs: Comparative Evidence from a Two-Country Study." In B. Hall, M. Doms, and F. Kramarz, eds., *Economics of Innovation and New Technology*. Washington, D.C.: National Academy Press.

Blanchflower, D. G., and R. Freeman. 1992. "Unionism in the United States and Other Advanced OECD Countries." *Industrial Relations* 31(1): 56–79.

_____. 1996. "Growing into Work." Discussion Paper no 296. London School of Economics Centre for Economic Performance, London.

Blanchflower, D. G., and A. J. Oswald. 1988. "Internal and External Influences upon Pay Settlements." *British Journal of Industrial Relations* 26(3): 363–70.

_____. 1994. *The Wage Curve*. Cambridge, Mass.: MIT Press.

Blanchflower, D. G., N. Millward, and A. J. Oswald. 1991. "Unionism and Employment Behaviour." *Economic Journal* 101: 815–34.

Blau, F. D., and L. M. Kahn. 1996. "International Differences in Male Wage Inequality: Institutions versus Market Forces." *Journal of Political Economy* 104(4): 791–837.

Bleaney, M. 1996. "Central Bank Independence, Wage-Bargaining Structure, and Macroeconomic Performance in OECD Countries." *Oxford Economic Papers* 48: 20–38.

Blyth, C. A. 1979. *Interaction between Collective Bargaining and Government Policies in Selected Member Countries*. Paris: Organisation for Economic Co-operation and Development.

Boal, W. M., and J. H. Pencavel. 1994. "The Effects of Labor Unions on Employment, Wages, and Days of Operation: Coal Mining in West Virginia." *Quarterly Journal of Economics* 109: 267–98.

Booth, A. 1995. *The Economics of the Trade Union*. Cambridge: Cambridge University Press.

Bronars, S. G., and D. R. Deere. 1986. "The Real and Financial Decisions of Unionized Firms in a Dynamic Setting." University of California at Santa Barbara. Processed.

Bronars, S. G., D. Deere, and J. Tracy. 1994. "The Effects of Unions on Firm Behavior: An Empirical Analysis Using Firm-level Data." *Industrial Relations* 33(4): 426–51.

Brown, C. 1990. "Firms' Choice of Method of Pay." *Industrial and Labor Relations Review* 43: 165S–182S.

Brown, J. N., and O. Ashenfelter. 1986. "Testing the Efficiency of Employment Contracts." *Journal of Political Economy* 94 (Supplement): S40–S87.

Brunello, G. 1992. "The Effect of Unions on Firms in Japanese Manufacturing." *Industrial and Labor Relations Review* 45: 471–487.

Bruno, M., and J. Sachs. 1985. *Economics of Worldwide Stagflation*. Cambridge, Mass. : Harvard University Press.

Butcher, K., and C. Rouse. 2001. "Wage Effects of Unions and Industrial Councils in South Africa." *Industrial and Labor Relations Review* 54(2): 349–74.

Calmfors, L. 1993. "Centralization of Wage Bargaining and Macroeconomic Performance: a Survey." Seminar Paper no. 536, Stockholm University, Institute for International Economic Studies.

Calmfors, L., and J. Driffill. 1988. "Bargaining Structure, Corporatism, and Macroeconomic Performance." *Economic Policy* 6: 13–62.

Cameron, D. R. 1984. "Social Democracy, Corporatism, Labour Quiescence, and the Representation of Interest in Advanced Capitalist Society." In J. H. Goldthorpe, ed., *Order and Conflict in Contemporary Capitalism*. Oxford: Oxford University Press.

Card, D. 1986. "Efficient Contracts with Costly Adjustment: Short-Run Employment Determination for Airline Mechanics." *American Economic Review* 76: 1045–71.

Christie, V. 1992. "Union Wage Effects and the Probability of Union Membership." *Economic Record* 68(200): 43–56.

Clark, K. B. 1984. "Unionization and Firm Performance: The Impact on Profits, Growth, and Productivity." *American Journal of Economics* 74: 893–919.

Connolly, R. A., B. T. Hirsch, and M. Hirschey. 1986. "Union Rent-Seeking, Tangible Capital, and Market Value of the Firm." *Review of Economics and Statistics* 68: 567–77.

Crouch, C. 1985. "Conditions for Trade Union Wage Restraint." In L. N. Lindberg and C. S. Maier, eds., *The Politics of Inflation and Economic Stagflation*. Washington, D.C.: The Brooking Institution.

_____. 1990. "Trade Unions in the Exposed Sector: Their Influence on Neo-corporatist Behavior." In R. Brunetta and C. Dell'Aringa, eds., *Labour Relations and Economic Performance*. New York: New York University Press.

Dabalen, A. 1998. "The Effect of Unions on Wages in South Africa: Repeated Cross-section Estimates." Working Paper. University of California, Berkeley.

Daniels, W. W. 1987. *Workplace Industrial Relations and Technological Change*. London: Frances Printer.

DeFina, R. 1983. "Unions, Relative Wages, and Economic Efficiency." *Journal of Labor Economics* 1(4): 408–29.

Denny, K. 1997. "Productivity and Trade Unions in British Manufacturing Industry 1973–85." *Applied Economics* 29: 1403–409.

Denny, K., and S. J. Nickell. 1991. "Unions and Investment in British Manufacturing Industry." *British Journal of Industrial Relations* 29: 113–22.

DiNardo, J. 1991. "Union Employment Effect: an Empirical Analysis." Discussion Paper no. 90-92-06. Department of Economics, University of California, Irvine.

Doiron, D. J., and W. C. Riddell. 1994. "The Impact of Unionization on Male-Female Earnings Differences in Canada." *Journal of Human Resources* 29(2): 504–34.

Dowrick, S. 1993. "Wage Bargaining Systems and Productivity Growth in OECD Countries." Background Paper no. 26. Australian Government Publishing Service, Canberra.

Duncan, G. J., and F. P. Stafford, 1980. "Do Union Members Receive Compensating Wage Differentials?" *American Economic Review* 70(3): 355–71.

Dunne, T., and D. MacPherson. 1994. "Unionism and Gross Employment Flows." *Southern Economic Journal* 60(3): 727–38.

Earle, J. S., and J. Pencavel. 1990. "Hours of Work under Trade Unionism." *Journal of Labor Economics* 8: 151–74

Elias P., and D. G. Blanchflower. 1989. "Occupations, Earnings, and Work Histories of Young Adults: Who Gets the Good Jobs?" Research Paper no. 68. Department of Employment, London.

Elliott, Kimberly Ann and Richard B. Freeman. 2001. "Global Labor Standards and Free Trade: The Siamese Twins of the Global Economy." Prepared for conference, The Impact on Health of Global Inequalities at Work, Harvard University Center for Society and Health, Boston, Mass., 20–22 June.

Faith, R. L., and J. D. Reid. 1987. "An Agency Theory of Unionism." *Journal of Economic Behavior and Organization* 8: 39–60.

Farber, H. S., and A. B. Krueger. 1992. "Union Membership in the United States: the Decline Continues." National Bureau of Economic Research Working Paper no. 4216. Cambridge, Mass.

Fields, G., and H. Wan, Jr. 1989. "Wage-Setting Institutions and Economic Growth." *World Development* 17: 1471–83.

Fields, G. S. 1994. "Changing Labor Market Conditions and Economic Development in Hong Kong, the Republic of Korea, Singapore, and Taiwan, China." *The World Bank Economic Review* 8(3): 395–414.

Filer, R. K., D. S. Hamermesh, and A. E. Rees. 1996. *The Economics of Work and Pay, 6th edition.* New York: HarperCollins College Publishers.

Flanagan, R. 1999. "Macroeconomic Performance and Collective Bargaining: An International Perspective." *Journal of Economic Literature* XXXVII: 1150–75.

Freeman, R. B. 1980a. "The Exit-Voice Tradeoff in the Labor Market: Unionism, Job Tenure, Quits, and Separations." *Quarterly Journal of Economics* 94(4): 643–74.

_____. 1980b. "Unionism and the Dispersion of Wages." *Industrial and Labour Relations Review* 34(1): 3–23.

_____. 1985. "Unions, Pensions, and Union Pension Funds." In D. Wise, ed., *Pensions, Labor, and Individual Choice.* Chicago: University of Chicago Press.

_____. 1986. "Unionism Comes to the Public Sector." *Journal of Economic Literature* 24: 41–85.

_____. 1988a. "Labour Market Institutions and Economic Performance." *Economic Policy* 3: 64–78.

_____. 1988b. "Union Density and Economic Performance, an Analysis of US States." *European Economic Review* 32: 707–16.

_____. 1993a. "Does Suppression of Labor Contribute to Economic Success? Labor Relations and Markets in East Asia." Working Paper, Harvard University, Department of Economics. Cambridge, Mass.

_____. 1993b. "Labor Markets and Institutions in Economic Development." *American Economic Review, Papers and Proceedings* 83(2): 403–09.

Freeman, R. B., and J. L. Medoff. 1979. "The Two Faces of Unionism." *Public Interest* 57: 69–93.

_____. 1984. *What do Unions do?* New York: Basic Books.

Freeman, R. B., and M. Kleiner. 1990. "The Impact of New Unionization on Wages and Working Conditions." *Journal of Labor Economics* 8(1): 8–25.

Frenkel, S. 1993. "Variations in Patterns of Trade Unionism: A Synthesis." In Frenkel, S., ed. *Organized Labor in the Asia-Pacific Region: A Comparative Study of Trade Unionism in Nine Countries*. Cornell International Industrial and Labor Relations Report no. 24. New York: ILR Press.

Garrett, G., and P. Lange. 1986. "Economic Growth in Capitalist Democracies." *World Politics* 38: 517–45.

Golden, M. 1993. "The Dynamics of Trade Unionism and National Economic Performance." *American Political Science Review* 87(2): 439–54.

Grant, E. K., R. Swidinsky, and J. Vanderkamp. 1987. "Canadian Union/Nonunion Wage Differentials." *Industrial and Labor Relations Review* 41(1): 93–107.

Green, D. A. 1991. "A Comparison of Estimation Approaches of Union/Nonunion Wage Differentials." Discussion Paper no. 91–13. Department of Economics, University of British Columbia, Vancouver.

Green, F. 1988. "The Trade Union Wage Gap in Britain: Some Recent Estimates." *Economics Letters* 27: 183–7.

_____. 1995. "Union Recognition and Paid Holiday Entitlement." Discussion Paper no. E95/13. University of Leeds, School of Business and Economic Studies. Leeds, United Kingdom.

Green, F., G. Hadjimatheou, and R. Smail. 1985. "Fringe Benefit Distribution in Britain." *British Journal of Industrial Relations* 23(2): 261–80.

Gregg, P., S. Mashin, and S. Szymanski. 1993. "The Disappearing Relationship between Directors' Pay and Corporate Performance." *British Journal of Industrial Relations* 24: 215–32.

Grout, P. A. 1984. "Investment and Wages in the Absence of Binding Contracts." *Economica* 52(4): 449–60.

Gunderson, M. 1982. "Union Impact on Wages, Fringe Benefits, and Productivity." In M. Gunderson and J. Anderson, eds., *Union-Management Relations in Canada*. Toronto: Addison-Wesley.

Gunderson, M., A. Ponak, and D. G. Taras, eds. 2000. *Union-Management Relations in Canada*, 4th ed. Toronto: Addison Wesley Longman.

Harcort, J. C. 1997. "Pay Policy, Accumulation and Productivity." *Economic and Labour Relations Review* 8: 78–89.

Heitger, B. 1987. "Corporatism, Technological Gaps and Growth in OECD Countries." *Weltwirtschaftliches Archiv* 123: 463–73.

Henley, A., and Euclid Tsakalotos. 1993. *Corporatism and Economic Performance*. Aldershot, U.K.: Edward Elgar.

Herzenberg, S. A. 1990 [Dec. 12–13]. "Introduction to Labor Standards and De-velopment in the Global Economy." Papers presented at the Symposium on Labor Standards and Development. Bureau of International Labor Affairs, U.S. Department of Labor, Washington, D.C.

Hibbs, D. 1978. "On the Political Economy of Long-Run Trends in Strike Activity." *British Journal of Political Science* 8: 153–75.

Hicks, J. R. 1932. *The Theory of Wages*. London: MacMillan Press.

Hirsch, B. T. 1990. "Innovative Activity, Productivity Growth, and Firm Performance: Are Labor Unions a Spur or a Deterrent?" In A. N. Link and V. K. Smith, eds., *Advances in Applied Microeconomics*. Greenwich, Conn.: JAI Press.

ILO (International Labour Organisation). 1997. *World Labour Report, Industrial Relations, Democracy, and Social Stability*. Geneva: ILO.

Jackman, R. 1993. "Mass Unemployment: International Experience and Lessons for Policy." Discussion Paper no.152. Centre for Economic Performance, London School of Economics, London.

Jackman, R., C. Pissarides, and S. Savouri. 1990. "Labour Market Policies and Unemployment in the OECD." *Economic Policy* 11: 449–90.

Johnson, H. G., and P. Mieszkowski. 1970. "The Effects of Unionisation on the Distribution of Income: A General Equilibrium Approach." *Quarterly Journal of Economics* 84(4): 539–61.

Karier, T. 1988. "New Evidence on the Effect of Unions and Imports on Monopoly Power." *Journal of Post Keynesian Economics* 10(3): 414–27.

Katz, H. C., T. A. Kochan, and K. R. Gobeille. 1983. "Industrial Relations Performance, Economic Performance, and QWL Performance: An Interplant Analysis." *Industrial and Labor Relations Review* 37: 3–17.

Keefe, J. H. 1992. "Do Unions Hinder Technological Change?" In L. Mishel and P. B. Voos, eds., *Unions and Economic Competitiveness*. New York: M. E. Sharpe.

Kennan, John. 1986. "The Economics of Strikes." In O. Ashenfelter and R. Layard, eds., *Handbook of Labor Economics*. Volume 2. Handbooks in Economics series, no. 5, Amsterdam; Oxford and Tokyo: North-Holland.

Kim, H. 1993. "The Korean Union Movement in Transition." In S. Frenkel, ed., *Organized Labor in the Asia-Pacific Region: A Comparative Study of Trade Unionism in Nine Countries*. Cornell International Industrial and Labor Relations Report no. 24. Ithaca, New York: ILR Press.

Knight, K. G. 1989. "Labour Productivity and Strike Activity in British Manufacturing Industries: Some Quantitative Evidence." *British Journal of Industrial Relations* 2793: 365–74.

Kornfeld, R. 1993. "The Effects of Union Membership on Wages and Employee Benefits: The Case of Australia." *Industrial and Labor Relations Review* 47(1): 114–28.

Krueger, A. O. 1993. *Political Economy of Policy Reform in Developing Countries.* Cambridge, Mass.: MIT Press.

Kupferschmidt, M., and R. Swidensky. 1989. "Longitudinal Estimates of the Union Effect on Wages, Wage Dispersion, and Pension Fringe Benefits." University of Guelph, Ontario, Canada. Processed.

Kusago, T., and Z. Tzannatos. 1998. "Export Processing Zones: A Review in Need of Update." World Bank, Social Protection Discussion Paper Series no, 9802. World Bank, Washington, D.C.

Lalonde, R. J., G. Marschke, and K. Troske. 1996. "Using Longitudinal Data on Establishments to Analyze the Effects of Union Organizing Campaigns in the United States." *Annales d' Economy et de Statistique* 41/42: 155–86.

Lange, P., and G. Garrett. 1985. "The Politics of Growth: Strategic Interaction and Economic Performance in the Advanced Industrial Democracies, 1974–1980." *Journal of Politics* 47(3): 792–827.

Latreille, P. 1992. "Unions and the Inter-Establishment Adoption of New Microelectronic Technologies in the British Private Manufacturing Sector." *Oxford Bulletin of Economics and Statistics* 54(1): 31–51.

Layard, R., S. Nickell, and R. Jackman. 1991. *Unemployment.* Oxford: Oxford University Press.

Lehmbruch, G. 1984. "Concentration and the Structure of Corporatist Networks." In J. H. Goldthorpe, ed., *Order and Conflict in Contemporary Capitalism.* Oxford: Clarendon Press.

Leonard, J. S. 1992. "Unions and Employment Growth." *Industrial Relations* 31(1): 80–94.

Levine, R., and D. Renelt. 1992. "A Sensitivity Analysis of Cross-Country Growth Regressions." *American Economic Review* 82(4): 942–63.

Lewis, H. G. 1986. *Union Relative Wage Effects: A Survey.* Chicago: University of Chicago Press.

_____. 1990. "Union/Non-union Wage Gaps in the Public Sector." *Journal of Labor Economics* 8(1): 260–327.

Lijphard, A., and M. Crepaz. 1991. "Corporatism and Consensus Democracy in Eighteen Countries: Conceptual and Empirical Linkages." *British Journal of Political Science* 21: 235–46.

Lindbeck, A., and D. J. Snower. 1989. "Macroeconomic Policy and Insider Power." *American Economic Review* 79(2): 370–76.

Long, R. J. 1993. "The Effect of Unionisation on Employment Growth of Canadian Companies." *Industrial and Labor Relations Review* 46(4): 81–93.

MacCurdy, T. E., and J. H. Pencavel. 1986. "Testing between Competing Models of Wage and Employment Determination in Unionized Markets." *Journal of Political Economy* 94 (Supplement): S3–S39.

MacDonald, G. M. 1983. "The Size and Structure of Union/Non-union Wage Differentials in Canadian Industry: Corroboration, Refinement and Extensions." *Canadian Journal of Economics* 16: 480–85.

MacDonald, G. M., and J. C. Evans. 1981. "The Size and Structure of Union/Non-union Wage Differentials in Canada." *Canadian Journal of Economics* 14: 216–31.

Machin, S., and S. Wadhwani. 1991. "The Effect of Unions on Organisational Change and Employment." *Economic Journal* 101: 835–54.

Machin, S., M. B. Stewart, and J. Van Reenen. 1993. "The Economic Effect of Multi-unionism: Evidence from the 1984 Workplace Industrial Relations Survey." *Scandinavian Journal of Economics* 95(3): 279–96.

Main, B. 1991. "The Union Relative Wage Gap." In D. Gallie, R. Penn, and M. Rose, eds., *Trade Unionism in Recession*. Oxford: Oxford University Press.

Main, B., and B. Reilly. 1992. "Women and the Union Wage Gap." *Economic Journal* 102: 49–66.

Malcomson, J. M. 1983. "Trade Unions and Economic Efficiency." *Economic Journal* 93 (Conference Papers Supplement): 52–65.

Martinello, F., and R. Meng. 1992. "Effects of Labor Legislation and Industry Characteristics on Union Coverage in Canada." *Industrial and Labor Relations Review* 46(1): 176–90.

Maskus, E., T. J. Rutherford, and S. Selby. 1995. "Implications of Changes in Labor Standards: A Computational Analysis for Mexico." *North American Journal of Economics & Finance* 6(2): 171–88.

Mazumdar, A. 1993. "Microeconomic Issues of Labor Markets in Developing Countries: Analysis and Policy Implications." EDI Seminar Paper 40. World Bank, Washington D.C.

McCallum, J. 1983. "Inflation and Social Consensus in the 1970s." *Economic Journal* 93: 784–805.

_____. 1986. "Unemployment in OECD Countries in the 1980s." *Economic Journal* 96: 942–60.

McDonald, I. M., and R. M. Solow. 1981. "Wage Bargaining and Employment." *American Economic Review* 71: 896–908.

McGuire, J. 1996. "Labor Movement Strength and Human Development in East Asia and Latin America." Presented at the 92nd Annual Meeting of the American Political Science Association, San Francisco, Calif. Processed.

Metcalf, D. 1993. "Industrial Relations and Economic Performance." London School of Economics Discussion Paper no. 129. Centre for Economic Performance.

Metcalf, D., and M. Stewart. 1992. "Closed Shops and Relative Pay: Institutional Arrangements or High Density." *Oxford Bulletin of Economics and Statistics* 54(4): 503–16

Miller, P., and C. Mulvey. 1991. "Australian Evidence on the Exit/Voice Model of the Labor Market." *Industrial and Labor Relations Review* 45: 44–47.

_____. 1993. "What Do Australian Unions Do?" *Economic Record* 69: 315–42.

Mishel, L. 1986. "The Structural Determinants of Union Bargaining Power." *Industrial and Labor Relations Review* 40(1): 90–105.

Moene, K. O., and M. Wallerstein. 1993a. "The Economic Performance of Different Bargaining Institutions: A Survey of the Theoretical Literature." *Wirtschaft und Gesellschaft* 19(4): 423–50.

_____. 1993b. "Egalitarian Wage Policies." Los Angeles: University of California. Processed.

_____. 1993c. "Technical Progress, Wage Compression, and the Centralization of Collective Bargaining." Los Angeles: University of California. Processed.

Moll, P. 1993. "Black South African Unions: Relative Wage Effects in International Perspective." *Industrial and Labor Relations Review* 46(2): 245–62.

Moreton, D. 1993. "Trade Union Effects on Labour Productivity in UK Manufacturing, 1950–87." London: University of Greenwich. Processed.

Mulvey, C. 1976. "Collective Agreements and Relative Earnings in UK Manufacturing in 1973." *Economica* 43: 419–27.

_____. 1986. "Wage Levels: Do Unions Make a Difference?" In J. Niland, ed., *Wage Fixation in Australia*. Sydney: Allen and Unwin.

Muramatsu, K. 1984. "The Effect of Trade Unions on Productivity in Japanese Manufacturing Industries." In M. Aoki, ed., *The Economic Analysis of the Japanese Firm*. Amsterdam: Elsevier Science Publishers, North Holland.

Murphy, K. M., A. Schleifer, and R. W. Vishy. 1993. "Why Is Rent-Seeking So Costly to Growth?" *American Economic Review, Papers and Proceedings* 83(2): 409–14.

Nakumura, K., H. Sato, and T. Kamiya. 1988. *Do Labor Unions Really Have a Useful Role?* Tokyo: Sago Rodo Kenkyujo.

Nelson, J. M. 1991. "Organized Labor, Politics, and Labor Market Flexibility in Developing Countries." *World Bank Research Observer* 6(1): 37–56.

Newell, A., and J. S. V. Symons. 1987. "Corporatism, Laissez-faire, and the Rise of Unemployment." *European Economic Review* 31: 567–614.

Nickell, S. J. 1997. "Unemployment and Labor Market Rigidities: Europe versus North America." *Journal of Economic Perspectives* 11(3): 55–74.

Nickell, S. J., and R. Layard. 1999. "Labour Market Institutions and Economic Performance." In O. Ashenfelter and D. Card, eds., *Handbook of Labor Economics, Vol. 3C*. Amsterdam; Oxford: North Holland.

Nickell, S. J., S. Wadhawani, and M. Wall. 1989. "Unions and Productivity Growth in Britain, 1974–86 Evidence from Company Accounts Data." Working Paper no. 1149. London School of Economics, Centre for Labour Economics. London, United Kingdom.

OECD (Organisation for Economic Co-operation and Development). 1988. "Employment and Unemployment." *Economic Outlook* 43 (June): 31–41. Paris: OECD.

_____. 1994. *Employment Outlook.* Paris: OECD.

_____. 1996. *Trade, Employment, and Labour Standards: a Study of Core Workers' Rights and International Trade.* Paris: OECD.

_____. 1997. *Employment Outlook.* Paris: OECD.

Olson, M. 1982. *The Rise and Decline of Nations: Economic Growth, Stagflation, and Social Rigidities.* New Haven: Yale University Press.

Osawa, M. 1989. "The Service Economy and Industrial Relations in Small and Medium-Size Firms in Japan." *Japan Labor Bulletin* 1: 1–10.

Oswald, A. J. 1993. "Efficient Contracts Are on the Labour Demand Curve: Theory and Facts." *Labour Economics* 1(1): 85–113.

Oswald, A. J., and P. J. Turnbull. 1985. "Pay and Employment Determination in Britain: What Are Labour Contracts Really Like?" *Oxford Review of Economic Policy* 1: 80–97.

Oswald, A. J., and I. Walker. 1993. "Rethinking Labour Supply: Contract Theory and Unions." London School of Economics. Centre for Economic Performance. Processed

Palley, T. I. 1999. "The Beneficial Effect of Core Labor Standards on Economic Growth." Technical Working Paper no. 10, AFL-CIO, Public Policy Department, Washington, D.C.

Panagides, A., and H. A. Patrinos. 1994. "Union/Non-union Wage Differentials in the Developing World: A Case Study of Mexico." Policy Research Working Paper 1269. World Bank, Washington, D.C.

Park, Y. 1991. "Union/Non-union Wage Differentials in the Korean Manufacturing Sector." *International Economic Journal* 5(4): 70–91.

Patrinos, H. A., and C. Sakellariou. 1992. "North American Indians in the Canadian Labour Market: a Decomposition of Wage Differentials." *Economics of Education Review* 11(3): 257–66.

Pencavel, J. H. 1991. *The Origins of Trade Union Power.* Oxford: Oxford University Press.

_____. 1995. "The Role of Labor Unions in Fostering Economic Development." Policy Research Working Paper no. 1469. World Bank, Washington, D.C.

Perez-Lopez, J. F. 1988. "Conditioning Trade on Foreign Labor Law: The U. S. Approach." *Comparative Labor Law Journal* 9(2): 253–292.

_____. 1990. "Worker Rights in the U. S. Omnibus Trade and Competitiveness Act." *Labor Law Journal* 41(4).

Perloff, J. M., and R. C. Sickles. 1987. "Union Wage, Hours, and Earnings Differentials in the Construction Industry." *Journal of Labor Economics* 5: 174–210.

Polachek, S., and W. S. Siebert. 1993. *The Economics of Earnings.* Cambridge: Cambridge University Press.

Rama, M. 1994. "Bargaining Structure and Economic Performance in the Open Economy." *European Economic Review* 38(2): 403–15.

_____. 1995. "Do Labor Market Policies and Institutions Matter? The Adjustment Experience in Latin America and the Caribbean." *Labour* (Special issue): 243–68.

_____. 1997a. "Organized Labor and the Political Economy of Product Market Distortions." *World Bank Economic Review* 11(2): 327–55.

_____. 1997b. "Trade Unions and Economic Performance: East Asia and Latin America." In J. W. McGuire, ed., *Rethinking Development in East Asia and Latin America.* University of Southern California, Center for International Studies.

_____. 1998. "Unions and Employment Growth: Evidence from Jamaica." Working Paper. World Bank, Washington, D.C.

Rama, M., and G. Tabellini. 1998. "Lobbying by Capital and Labor over Trade and Labor Market Policies." *European Economic Review* 42(7): 1295–316.

Ravn, M., and J. R. Sørensen. 1997. "Minimum Wages: Curse or Blessing." *Research in Labor Economics* 16: 343–68.

Rees, A. 1963. "The Effects of Unions on Resource Allocation." *Journal of Law and Economics* 6: 69–78.

Reynolds, M. 1986. "Trade Unions in the Production Process Reconsidered." *Journal of Political Economy* 94: 443–47.

Robinson, C., and N. Tomes. 1984. "Union Wage Differentials in the Public and Private Sectors: A Simultaneous Equation Specification." *Journal of Labor Economics* 2: 106–27.

Rowthorn, R. E. 1992a. "Centralization, Employment, and Wage Dispersion." *Economic Journal* 102: 506–23.

_____. 1992b. "Corporatism and Labour Market Performance." In J. Pekkarinen, M. Pohjola, and R. Rowthorn, eds., *Social Corporatism: A Superior Economic System*. Oxford: Clarendon Press.

_____. 1995. "Capital Formation and Unemployment." *Oxford Review of Economic Policy* 11(1): 26–39.

Sapsford, D., and Z. Tzannatos. 1993. *The Economics of the Labour Market*. London: MacMillan Press.

Scarpetta, S. 1996. "Assessing the Role of Labour Market Policies and Institutional Settings on Unemployment: A Cross-Country Study." *OECD Economic Studies* 26: 43–98.

Schmidt, C. 1995. "Relative Wage Effects of German Unions." Selapo: University of Munich. Processed.

Schmidt, C., and K. F. Zimmermann. 1991. "Work Characteristics, Firm Size, and Wages." *Review of Economics and Statistics* 73: 705–10.

Schmitter, P. C. 1981. "Interest Intermediation and Regime Governability in Contemporary Western Europe and North America." In S. Berger, ed., *Organising Interests in Western Europe*. Cambridge: Cambridge University Press.

Schnabel, C. 1991. "Trade Unions and Productivity: the German Evidence." *British Journal of Industrial Relations* 29: 15–24.

Siebert, S., and J. Addison. 1981. "Are Strikes Accidental?" *Economic Journal* 91: 389–404.

Simpson, W. 1985. "The Impact of Unions on the Structure of Canadian Wages: An Empirical Analysis with Microdata." *Canadian Journal of Economics* 18(1): 164–81.

Soskice, D. 1990. "Wage Determination: The Changing Role of Institutions in Advanced Industrialized Countries." *Oxford Review of Economic Policy* 6(4): 36–61.

Standing, G. 1992. "Do Unions Impede or Accelerate Structural Adjustment? Malaysia Industrial versus Company Unions in an Industrializing Labour Market." *Cambridge Journal of Economics* 16: 327–54.

Stevens, M., N. Millward, and D. Smart., 1989. "Trade Union Membership and the Closed Shop in 1989." *Employment Gazette* November: 615–23.

Stewart, M. B. 1983. "Relative Earnings and Individual Union Membership in the UK." *Economica* 50: 111–25.

_____. 1987. "Collective Bargaining Arrangements, Closed Shops, and Relative Pay." *The Economic Journal* 97: 140–56.

Stewart, M. B. 1990. "Union Wage Differentials, Product Market Influence, and the Division of Rents." *The Economic Journal* 100: 1122–37.

_____. 1991. "Union Wage Differentials in the Face of Changes in the Economic and Legal Environment." *Economica* 58: 155–72.

_____. 1995. "Union Wage Differentials in an Era of Declining Unionization." *Oxford Bulletin of Economics and Statistics* 57(2): 143–66.

Tarantelli, E. 1986. "The Regulation of Inflation and Unemployment." *Industrial Relations* 25(1): 1–15.

Teal, F. 1996. "The Size and Source of Economic Rents in a Developing Country Manufacturing Labour Market." *The Economic Journal* 106: 963–76.

Tzannatos, Z. 1996. "Labor Policies and Regulatory Regimes." In Claudio Frischtak, ed., *Regulatory Policies and Reform: A Comparative Perspective*. Washington, D.C.: World Bank.

Trejo, S. J. 1993. "Overtime Pay, Overtime Hours, and Labor Unions." *Journal of Labor Economics* 11: 253–78.

Ulph, A., and D. Ulph. 1989. "Labor Markets and Innovations." *Journal of the Japanese and International Economics* 3(4): 395–405.

_____. 1990. "Union Bargaining: A Survey of Recent Work." In D. Sapsford and Z. Tzannatos, eds., *Current Issues in Labour Economics*. London: MacMillan Press.

van Reenen, J. 1993. "The Creation and Capture of Rents: Wages, Market Structure, and Innovations in UK Manufacturing Firms." University College, London, Department of Economics. Processed.

Visser, J. 1990. "In Search of Inclusive Unionism." *Bulletin of Comparative Labour Relations* 18: 15–24.

Wagner, J. 1991. "Gewerkschaftmitgliedschaft und Arbeitseinkommen in der Bundesrepublik Deutschland." *Ifo Student* 109–140.

World Bank. 1993. *The East Asian Miracle: Economic Growth and Public Policy*. Oxford: Oxford University Press.

_____. 1995. *World Development Report 1995*. Oxford: Oxford University Press.

Yaron, G. 1990. "Trade Unions and Women's Relative Pay: A Theoretical and Empirical Analysis Using UK Data." Applied Economics Discussion Paper no. 95. Oxford University, Institute for Economics and Statistics. Oxford, United Kingdom.

Zweimuller, J., and E. Barth. 1994. "Bargaining Structure, Wage Determination, and Wage Dispersion in Six OECD Countries." *Kyklos* 47: 81–93.

Index

Australia: bargaining coordination in, 90; and job turnover and job tenure, 9, 65; wage markup in, 7, 43, 46, 49

Austria: bargaining coordination in, 90; wage markup in, 44, 46

Bargaining coordination: aspects of, 11, 84, 85; and corporatism, 35–36; country rankings based on alternative valuations of, 89–90; and dispute resolution, 36–37; and economic performance, 12–13, 98–107, 120; explanation of, 11–12, 145; formal, 108–109; forms of, 79; and global environment, 14; indicators of, 84–90, 121–131; and industrial relations, 13; informal, 11, 13, 35, 85, 108–109, 120; measurement of, 84; and political orientation of government, 13; and strikes, 116; and substudies of economic outcomes, 133–142; and union concentration, 11, 33–35; and union density and coverage, 111–115. *See also* Collective bargaining

Bargaining coverage: and bargaining coordination, 111–115; and economic performance, 11, 99; explanation of, 11, 81, 145; in selected OECD countries, 81–83; and unemployment, 13, 120; and union density, 94–98, 111–115; and wage markup, 46–47

Bargaining level: and bargaining coordination, 11, 85; and centralized collective bargaining, 89, 90; explanation of, 146; and wage markup, 58–59

Belgium: bargaining coordination in, 90; multiunionism in, 33

Canada: bargaining coordination in, 90; technology use in, 72; union density in, 57; wage markup in, 7, 8, 43, 44, 50–52

Centralized collective bargaining: and bargaining levels, 89, 90; costs and benefits of, 30–31; and economic performance, 32, 103; explanation of, 28–29; and internalization of externalities, 29, 32, 34; and wage demands, 29; and wage drift, 32–33

China, economic growth and labor standards in, 19